Unhappy

Mother's

Day

Unhappy Mother's Day

Cheryl Cook

WOODSONG
PUBLISHING

Seymour, IN

Unhappy Mother's Day
Cheryl Cook

Copyright 2022

All Scripture quotations are from the King James Version of the Bible.

All rights reserved. This publication may not be reproduced, stored in an electronic system, or transmitted in any form or by any means, electronic, mechanical, photocopy, recording, or otherwise, without proper credit to the author. Brief quotations may be used without permission.

ISBN 979-8-9855200-4-0

Cover Design by Jeremy Hart for Hart Creative + Design

Published by Woodsong Publishing

Printed in the United States of America.

Dedication

This book is dedicated to two special people in my life. Stan and Benjamin you are my world, and I feel so honored to love and be loved by you.

Stan, you walked every inch of this 12 1/2 year road and seemed that you never wavered or gave up. We saw some mighty rough storms and some terribly lonely nights, but because you believed I found the courage to believe also. You made me so mad when I had a bad attitude and you wouldn't let me stay that way, always reasoned it out or talked me out of it, and I love you for it. You have always been my protector, and your love always surrounded me. I love you, and I can't see me without you.

Benji, you have grown from that baby that I couldn't stop kissing his curly head, to that grown man who has a wife and a baby himself. You will never know how much I love you. I prayed so long for you, and you finally found me. You have brought so much joy to our lives, I would have never felt complete without your love. I thank God every day for you. It really is true: you didn't grow under my heart, you grew in it.

Table Of Contents

In The Beginning

Dreams And Plans

Can I Be Like Them?

Don't Be Jealous, Hannah

Rachel, It's Not Your Fault

Wait For It, Sarah

Who Are You?

Tick Tock, Elizabeth

My Miracle Is Here!

Chapter 1

In The Beginning

UNHAPPY MOTHER'S DAY

No calling is greater, nobler, or more fulfilling than that of motherhood.
—Sally Clarkson

God's word has so many wonderful passages in it and life changing nuggets that just leap out and grab a person. There are times when I'm reading along and honestly not really expecting to learn anything new, or just reading so I can mark off another day in my Bible chart, and out of nowhere, like a bolt of lightning, God gives me a life and spirit changing revelation. It may not mean a thing to anyone else, but to me it reframed my whole mind set. That very thing happened unexpectedly the other day while writing this book. In one of the services I was in, a preacher quoted John 1:1, "In the beginning was the Word, and the Word was with God, and the Word was God." He then said, "If you ever got a word from Him or ever read His word, He will be faithful. Every word he promised He will deliver." I have read the book of John dozens of times and probably have heard a version of it preached a dozen and one, but the awesomeness of it struck me. Down through the ages He has never failed to be faithful, and more than that, He will always be. I received a word of faith years ago about being a mother, and through the years of waiting I forgot it or was so deep in my own self-pity that I buried it. You can never bury God's Word deep enough that it gets lost. He has a way of bringing it not only to the surface, but placing it smack in the middle of our hearts and minds. I buried my promise. What have you buried?

I have found that God never bargains. His word is true

In The Beginning

and unchanging, and the only alterations that are made are to the person reading it. He won't change truth just because you don't want to be different. I have been stubborn and tried to bargain with God over several issues, but it all has boiled down to me realizing He always wants what is best for me. Once I realized that, my worry and restlessness was put to bed, and sweet peace filled my life. When I longed for and begged God for a baby, I thought I would make a deal with Him. He gives me what I want, and I live for Him. I mean 'go all in' live for Him. It normally takes two to bargain, but I didn't hold up my end of the faithfulness bargain many times. On the surface I was serving God, but deep in my heart I wasn't where I should be and knew it. No one could tell, but I was a mess of wanting to be totally devoted and just give up, but He gave me a word several years ago, and stuck by me even at my worst.

This is a story of faithfulness. Not mine. His. The second stanza of the beautiful old hymn written by Thomas Chisholm says, "Great is Thy faithfulness! Great is Thy faithfulness! Morning by morning new mercies I see. All I have needed Thy hand hath provided. Great is Thy faithfulness, Lord unto me!" The last stanza is even more appropriate to my situation: "Pardon for sin and a peace that endureth, Thine own dear presence to cheer and to guide; Strength for today, and bright hope for tomorrow Blessing all mine, with ten thousand beside." I would have to hold on to those words for many years, but "blessing all mine, with ten thousand beside," finally arrived.

I want to tell you a story about a very dark time in my life. A season of ups and downs, joys and sorrows, warmth and a chill to the bone. As my journey begins, you can follow me on this rollercoaster ride called infertility. It was

UNHAPPY MOTHER'S DAY

such a beautiful day. The birds were singing, the sun was shining down, and the gentle breeze was blowing the flowers and newly planted shrubs and trees. Oh, how I have always loved spring in Missouri! Not too hot, not too cold. I could open the windows and let the fresh breeze sweep through the house. Even a grumpy spirit can't stay down long in the spring. It was just a 'perfect' day. I had the day off and was planning on shopping with friends, lunch, and then relaxing in my little house with my poodle, Tiger, by my side. Maybe throwing in some sewing and Cardinal baseball. Absolutely nothing could ruin this day for me. I thought about Revelation 21:5 that said, "And he that sat upon the throne said, Behold, I make all things new. And he said unto me, Write: for these words are true and faithful." That's what spring feels like to me, everything is new and fresh, and He is faithful to give me that 'new.' I was content with my marriage, church, jobs, and friends, but I felt I needed a refreshing in my spirit. It was time not only to spring clean my house but also my life and attitude.

As I walked to the mailbox I thought about my life and the things I had yet to accomplish. I was right where I had always wanted to be. Working in the ministry by teaching at a Christian school. Coaching girls volleyball and sometimes just hanging with the high school kids I had grown to love. I went with my husband some weekends while he preached and sang, and I thoroughly enjoyed him and the churches. Right now life was just about perfect, but where would God take me? What else could I do for Him? I knew God would provide the means and answers if I just trusted and followed Him with my whole heart. He always did. Psalm 143:8 says what my heart meant, "Cause me to hear thy lovingkindness in the morning; for in thee do I trust: cause me to know the way wherein I should walk; for I lift up my soul unto thee." More than anything I wanted to walk with the Lord and

In The Beginning

follow Stan as he followed Jesus.

    I reached into the mailbox before going out that Saturday to get what was probably just junk mail, and in the midst of all the ads were a couple of envelopes. Maybe one of them was a letter from my parents in Louisiana. That was back in the dinosaur days when people wrote letters, not e-mails. I missed mom and dad so much, and I always loved getting mail from them! Mom's letters were newsy and fun, and no matter how rough the week had been, they lifted my spirits. Sure enough, to my delight, one was a letter from her. I couldn't wait to tear it open and read it, but the other envelope stopped me in my tracks. I recognized the return address as a friend from the church, who was expecting a baby. My stomach knotted up, and I felt sick. I wanted to just toss it in the trash and forget it even came, but that wouldn't do any good because they would just announce the baby shower at church come Sunday. Sure enough, it was a ridiculously cute baby shower announcement. How could one small piece of paper instantly cause so much dread and anger? I kept my attitude and anger under control, for only one thing could trigger such a reaction these days, and anything to do with a baby was certainly it. Immediately my eyes filled with tears and caused a little ire to rise up in me. I knew what was causing the anger but just couldn't seem to help myself. Jealousy, plain and simple. There was no way to sugar coat it. I was mad and felt forgotten and alone once again. I was mad at the girl having the baby, and I was mad at God. At that moment life just didn't seem fair, and my feelings toward her were totally unfair. Obviously the girl couldn't help being over the moon that she was pregnant. God had been better to me than I ever deserved, and I immediately felt ashamed of myself, but more than that, I was sad and angry and not quite ready to repent of those feelings. I had mastered the art of holding on to the

UNHAPPY MOTHER'S DAY

ugly feelings and hurt. I felt betrayed and lonely. So much for the feeling of contentment. I know these words, and the chapters that follow, are going to seem overly dramatic, but this is a raw, unfiltered, and piercing look into a bleak period of my life, followed by a miraculous gifting. Psalm 147:3 says, "He heals the broken hearted and binds up there wounds." It took a while for my heart to mend, but it did, and it was amazing. Are you struggling with a heartache? Do you have a promise that seems to have been forgotten by God? Are you in the storm of your life? Lift up your eyes and see your Savior. Singer Dolly Parton said, "The way I see it, if you want the rainbow, you gotta put up with the rain." Stay faithful and use the umbrella of prayer to cover you until you dance in the calm after the storm.

Baby showers. Oh how I hated those two words. I thought: How did such a depressing tradition even get started? Just have the baby and be done with it already. You don't have to make such a big deal out of it. I get the excitement, but it is normal and natural and doesn't have to be such a big event. Every shower just seemed to mock me and remind me of what I was missing. Shopping for the present was even worse. The cute little pajama sets, onesies, and booties threw me into a dismal state. When I first began the process of anticipating starting a family, I enjoyed them and dreamed about my own shower. The fun games and cute gifts. The anticipation and my 'bump.' It would be all about MY little blessing from above. I now know that the wrong attitude was all in my head, but the feelings were real. Shower after shower, year after year. I was one of the leaders in the church and was expected to participate, but how could I go again? I didn't have another happy face I could paint on. Some women I knew already had two children, and weren't all that happy about having a third. It really just didn't seem fair. Life right now just didn't seem fair. I just couldn't get

In The Beginning

past that saying, "life just didn't seem fair." That was my motto at the time, and the words played over and over in my head, like a recording. My heart was breaking in a million pieces while I smiled outside but wept on the inside. I only asked God for one favor. One tiny baby. That was all. Why, why, why? Now I didn't care about the birds, sun, or breeze. I allowed my 'perfect day' to be ruined all because of one routine trip to the mailbox and one envelope. Forget shopping, friends and lunch. I was going to stay inside the house and brood and feel sorry for myself. It was a terrible attitude, but right now I just didn't care. At that time I had no way of knowing that God had a perfect plan and saw me and loved me as I was. He made me and knew that deep in my heart I wasn't that ugly, hateful girl. If only I had paid more attention to Lamentations 3:25, "The Lord is good unto them that wait for Him, to the soul that seeketh Him." Learning to patiently wait on Him, and pray for His perfect will, would have made those lonely, bitter tears more bearable. Max Lucado said, "Our prayers may be awkward. Our attempts may be feeble. But since the power of prayer is in the One who hears it and not in the one who says it, our prayers do make a difference." I didn't mean to have a jealous heart, but it seemed unavoidable. It wasn't, but I was comfortable in my selfishness.

I had an amazing childhood growing up in the beautiful state of Michigan. I spent almost every weekend with my cousins either at my house or theirs, and our game of choice when we were young was almost always playing house. There were four of us, and I always got to be the mama because I was the oldest girl. Scott was the dad who grabbed his pretend briefcase and dutifully went off to work and did 'dad things.' Renee was younger, so she had dual roles. She was the perfect daughter who went to school, or she was the baby that just played around the house all day.

UNHAPPY MOTHER'S DAY

Michael was the older boy, so he was the grandpa or dog. He did whatever grandpas or dogs do. We had it perfectly worked out in our minds, and other than a few minor details here and there, it was almost always the same every time we got together. I mimicked my mama's persona and did what I thought she would do but actually had no idea of my parents real life. Each time I played house, my pretend families were exact. Each of us knew our roles and always played the parts to a T. As a child it was just like I thought life was supposed to be. Perfect. No matter who I played house with, I was married and always had children. The game's rules and dynamics rarely changed, only the players. I never dreamed that life wasn't like my uniquely crafted game of house. All of my parents' friends had children that I played with, so I never really paid attention to see if any of them were childless. It didn't matter though, because that was definitely not going to happen to me. I knew how the 'game of life' was played, and if I followed all the rules, the end result would be perfect. Children grew up, got married, had children, and that was that.

After growing up and getting married I soon found out that life was not one perpetual game of house, and in real life some couples' 'families' didn't include kids. Maybe intentionally or maybe not. That wasn't and still isn't my business. Why people take it upon themselves to pose the embarrassing and nosey "when are you having a baby" question to couples is beyond me. Most times it is uncalled for and hurtful. Some women choose careers over motherhood, which is fine. A few felt they weren't mother material, which is also fine, but some ladies like me craved a child but at the end of the day still had empty arms and cribs. I tried desperately to hold on to Matthew 21:22 that said, "And all things whatsoever you shall ask in prayer, believing, ye shall receive." Year after painful year, though

In The Beginning

the asking remained stedfast, the believing got a little harder to manage. So many times I doubted, but I tried to never let it take seed in my heart. Mark 11:23 gives us this promise: "For verily I say unto you, That whosoever shall say unto this mountain, Be thou removed, and be thou cast into the sea; and shall not doubt in his heart, but shall believe that those things which he saith shall come to pass; he shall have whatsoever he saith." Journalist and author Jane Clayson Johnson said, "It takes a lot of faith to put everything you have on the altar of God, trust in Him, and know that His plan is better for you than the plan you have mapped out for yourself." Sometimes God's plan does not include what you are praying for, and we have to acknowledge that it is okay and He must have something powerfully good planned for us. Proverbs 10:22 says, "The blessing of the Lord, it maketh rich, and he addeth no sorrow with it." The Benson Commentary explains, "Riches are gotten by God's favor and blessing. And adds content and comfort with them." I knew I was in God's hand and was going to wait 'patiently' for His blessing.

    As I grew from a little girl to a teenager, I still had it all planned out. I wanted the whole package: husband, career, fine things, and three kids: two girls and a boy. I was going to have it all, and they were going to be perfect. My mom made it look so easy. She juggled the blessings of marriage, job, three children and church activities, and I was going to do the same. I never dreamed she worked so hard. When I grew up, I realized that it was not that easy for everyone. Most lives are far from fairytale. I, along with other ladies I have met, have tried to master all four, but for me, one was missing. My missing element was the children part. I should have been happy with three of the four blessings, as some women only had one or two of those. As each year passed, I quoted the "Ask and ye shall receive" verse many

UNHAPPY MOTHER'S DAY

times over. I also memorized, "Children are an heritage from the Lord" (Psalm 127:3). See, I rationalized, it was inevitable. God said it in His word. I lived for Him, served and loved Him, and was going to have the perfect home life. Children and all. I never realized that I had forgotten one important fact. I completely left God out of my plans. I thought I was in complete control of my body, life, and future. I said I wanted His will, and I believe I really did, but I had no clue that it involved waiting over twelve years for a baby. But, He is always faithful. Isaiah 55:8 states, "For my thoughts are not your thoughts, neither are your ways my ways, saith the Lord."

Bishop T.D. Jakes put it like this, "Delayed does not mean denied. God is just giving you a moment of silence to prepare for what He's about to do in your life." I sure wish I would have taken heed to that statement. I've heard it said that when we ask questions of God, He has three answers: yes, no, and wait. When I assumed that by His silence the answer was "no," I threw my little fits. Now, many years later, I realize that the answer was actually "just wait." Had I been more mature in the Lord, I would have realized that He wanted the best for me, and the timing was all wrong. Now, years later, I am embarrassed by my thoughts and childish actions. I wish I would have memorized 1 Corinthians 13:11 sooner, "When I was a child, I spake as a child, I understood as a child, I thought as a child: but when I became a man, I put away childish things." I love what Diane Sowerby said in her Amazing Movement blog, "One day you will tell your story of how you overcame what you went through and it will be someone else's survival guide."

Chapter 2

Dreams and Plans

UNHAPPY MOTHER'S DAY

Mothering is the gospel lived out as you hold your child's heart in beauty, prayer, and patience. It's not the big decision, but the little ones, trusting God through it all.
—Elizabeth Hawn

Once upon a time in a kingdom far, far away lived a fair young maiden who met and fell in love with a handsome prince. They first became best friends, confided in each other, and shared their hopes and dreams. Soon they had a storybook wedding with many loyal subjects and family watching and cheering on the young royal couple. After a fairytale honeymoon they eagerly moved into their spacious, new castle. Soon, as planned, they welcomed their first new little one. A perfect, bouncing baby boy. Not much later two tiny, beautiful ladies were added. Their prince and princesses had arrived, and their lives and family were complete. Their children grew and became successful, and the couple grew old gracefully together. After many joy-filled, carefree years, the family lived happily ever after. The couple slew dragons and conquered kingdoms together. The End.

Well, all that sounds really nice, and it makes for a great story, but reality is sometimes not as beautiful or grand as a well written fairy tale. I had read so many of those Christian-romance stories when I was young, and I guess I had a false sense of reality. I suppose I really thought that 'adulting' would be the same way. I did find my handsome

Dreams And Plans

prince, Stanley Joe Cook, and after becoming best friends first, we fell in love. Dr. Seuss said, " You know you're in love when you can't fall asleep because reality is finally better than your dreams." After dating off and on for a few years, we had our version of a storybook wedding. August 9, 1986, was the most ideal Saturday ever. The weather was perfect for me but a bit too warm for my northern relatives who honored me with their presence. I still chuckle when I remember them grumbling about the heat. I was the one wearing the long white dress with four layers, not them! It could have been raining, sleeting, or hailing, but I didn't care, because I was excited to be marrying my true love and begin our world of dreams. Our wedding was beautiful and perfect for us and our budget. After all, we weren't real royalty! With friends and family present, my 'prince' sang a beautiful song to me, then we promised our love to each other. Pastor McGruder finished blessing our union with Mark 10:9: "What therefore God hath joined together, let not man put asunder." I was ready to begin our story.

Our mansion was actually just a small apartment right beside the Kennett fire station, which when the alarm sounded in the middle of the night, put us on the roof, but it was fine because we were married, in love, and ready to dive headlong into our future. Together we decided that our three wonderful fairytale children were going to have to wait a while. We had plenty of time and wanted to be more financially stable and enjoy each other first. Boy, waiting a while was an understatement! We began our marriage attempting to live by Matthew 6:33-34 which says, "But seek ye first the kingdom of God, and his righteousness; and all these things shall be added unto you. Take no thought of the morrow: for the morrow shall take thought for the things of itself. Sufficient unto the day is the evil thereof." The 'plenty of time' we thought we had turned into twelve

UNHAPPY MOTHER'S DAY

plus years, and that ended up seeming like an eternity. We did have a great life though, and every day was an adventure being married to my best friend. We were doing what we knew the Lord had planned for us, serving God together and loving life. We did seek the Lord first and were trying to "take no thought for the morrow," but the longer we waited for the added things, the more impatient we became.

Stan and I always vowed to put God first, and we sought to do His perfect will. Always. We began our life together with many plans and dreams as most newlyweds do. We married when I was twenty-one and Stan twenty-three, and we longed to be used in the ministry and raise a family who would serve and love Him. Our wedding theme was based on the second part of Ruth 1:16, "For whither thou goest, I will go; and where thou lodgest, I will lodge: thy people shall be my people, and thy God my God." Traveling for many years has seen us 'go' many places. Forty plus states and counting, with many, many lodging places from top notch to quaint (which sometimes means pretty rough). We have loved each other's family, and of course we both loved our God. The first few years were spent with Stan traveling, singing all over the country with the McGruder's, and I taught Monday through Friday at the local Christian school. Sunday school was my passion, and I began teaching 2-3 year olds. Those babies were so precious, like huggable, lovable little sponges. I eventually worked my way up to my favorites, the 8-9 year olds. They were so eager to learn God's word and not too cool yet to do the fun songs. I always loved children of all ages, and Stan was a "baby magnet." The kids of the church all called him Uncle Stan, and my school kids were all my babies. We had no idea at the time that all the interaction with those children was going to have to suffice for a while.

Dreams And Plans

Occasionally, when Stan was not singing with the group, we got to preach a weekend revival somewhere within driving distance, trying to always be home by Monday. That was a bit out of my comfort zone because I would rather be with people I already knew, but Stan was a natural. He had to nudge and encourage me to stretch and grow. We loved every time we got to minister out and envisioned someday adding a family to the mix. We didn't have much money, but we had God and each other with heads and hearts full of dreams. We had already been planning and knew that we wanted to wait at least two years before beginning a family. With God's help we wanted to be on the best financial and spiritual footing we could before adding a baby. Right then, though, with each of our ministries, we were having the time of our lives. We never tired of being with each other: listening to ballgames, playing games, or just laughing, planning and dreaming. " The secret to a happy marriage is finding the right person. You know they're right if you love to be with them all the time," quipped famous chef, Julia Child. And that summed up our life. We enjoyed each others company more than any one else's.

We were driving home from one of those late night preaching dates and began discussing our future baby plans. We had been married almost two years and felt that we were ready to take the big step of parenthood. After much prayer the decision had been made. Boy or girl, we just didn't care as long as it was healthy and happy. We had read Psalm 37:4-5, "Delight thyself also in the Lord; and He shall give thee the desires of thine heart. Commit thy way unto the Lord; trust also in Him; and He shall bring it to pass". We drove the rest of the way home in excitement and anticipation, holding hands and giggling as if we were keeping a big secret from the whole world. We decided to keep it just that, a secret, because we have always been private about that sort of thing,

UNHAPPY MOTHER'S DAY

and personally I feel that is no one else's business. God was the only one who knew about it and the last part of Psalm 44:21 says, "for he knoweth the secrets of the heart..." If He knows about it then it is already taken care of. After all, it would probably take a month or two to get pregnant, and I have seen many women make an early announcement just to be embarrassed when they were wrong. We sure didn't want to jump the gun with that. Boy, did we ever get the timing all wrong! For 12 1/2 years I'm not sure we even had a gun to jump. Pastor Dwight Fulton of the Bastrop United Pentecostal Church said one Sunday while preaching, "You won't always be strong, but you can always be faithful." There were many times where I felt weak in spirit but always tried to be faithful to my God, husband, and church.

We really were happy being a family of two, but as one year turned into two, we became a bit anxious. Most of our friends were adding their second child by now, and soon the unsolicited advice began trickling in. The old saying is true, "Advice not asked for is often not heeded." The advice was unwanted and unappreciated, because no one knew our desire (not even our parents at this time). Comments such as, "I just can't believe that you guys don't want children," or "I think you're doing the best thing by not having children," or "I wouldn't want to have a kid this day and age either" came rolling in. As I look back I notice that most of the people giving us their words of wisdom had children and didn't have to worry about empty arms. We both tried to act like it didn't bother us, smile, and sidestep the hurtful words. Or better yet we became great at making a joke out of it. MOST people really don't mean to hurt, they just feel the need to say something and invariably say the wrong thing. Anything that is different is sometimes uncomfortable, and a married couple without children in my world was definitely different. Married people having children is seen as a very

Dreams And Plans

normal thing, and we found out how hard it is to be abnormal in a normal world. What do you talk about when others are talking potty training, or loose teeth, or kindergarten? Again, I felt as if I were a foreigner trying my best to comprehend a language I had never learned. I imagined people looking at me like I had two heads. The entire chapter of Psalm 136 explains all of God's exploits and how He slew kings, brought the Israelites out of Egypt, and created this beautiful world for us to enjoy. So, why do I doubt? He can do anything. So, why do I doubt? He will never forsake us. So, why do I doubt? With an amazing God who obviously has all power, why in the world would I ever doubt His power to give me a baby? Verse 22 reassured me many times throughout the years: "Who remembered us in our low estate; for his mercy endureth forever." Whatever you're going through right now, He will remember you.

Finally, after about five unsuccessful years trying to conceive, we could no longer bear the pain alone and included our families and pastor in on our secret. I'm sure they all knew we were "trying" for a baby, because they knew how much we both loved children. We figured that with everyone praying on our behalf it was a lock, and we would be holding our angel soon. Our hopes were rekindled, and our faith was built up. But we were wrong again. We prayed and prayed but again, nothing. Thomas Merton said, "What is the use of praying if at the very moment of prayer, we have so little confidence in God that we are busy planning our own kind of answer to our prayer?" I was beginning again to get nervous, and I began to be afraid that I would never be a mother, and the questions began to roll in my mind. I could never be as good as my mom, or would I just be a terrible mom? Is that why? Would I even be able to love a baby enough, or be terribly selfish? Is that why? Was I meant to have empty arms forever? When these questions arose time and again,

UNHAPPY MOTHER'S DAY

I would rely on Deuteronomy 31:8: "And the Lord, he it is that doth go before thee; he will be with thee, he will not fail thee, neither forsake thee: fear not, neither be dismayed." I always knew He was with me, but the human part of me had a small nagging fear in the back of my mind. I knew He was never going to leave me, but I couldn't help but be anxious. Would He fail me? I had years of experience as He proved His faithfulness over and over, and I knew the answer but still asked that question every once in a while. One Sunday while listening to a sermon about Abraham, I heard the following nugget not only with my ears but also with my heart. When Abraham was asked to sacrifice Isaac, it took him three days to get to the mountain. That must have been an agonizing trip for him. Three days to think about the task at hand but also three days to burn every memory of Isaac in his mind. He never wanted to forget his boy, but what happened on that mountain was amazing. His miracle! Three days doesn't seem long to most people, but for Abraham it must have been an eternity. Sometimes it takes a while to get your miracle, but it is oh so worth the wait. What are you waiting for? Sometimes this trip called life is a long hard trek but hold fast to God and let Him be your guide. The journey will not seem so long with Him leading you.

A secret is not a secret as long as more than one person knows about it. Eventually, it seemed the whole world knew "our secret" and then came more unwanted comments, advice, and ribbing. Try this, try that, relax, pray, get medical help, and the list goes on and on. "Can't you figure it out?" "Don't you know what to do?" And the most hurtful and sobering was, "Maybe it just isn't meant to be." I know that people don't mean to appear calloused, and I'm sure I have been at times also, but one thing that season in my life taught me was to weigh my thoughts and

Dreams And Plans

measure my comments? Does each situation really call for my answer or joke? Sometimes silence is the best answer. Each comment made us feel as if we were defective, and what should have been easy and natural became anything but. I became abnormally focused on conceiving a child, and every disappointing month the pressure built. I felt that each month had to be the one, and when it wasn't I collapsed in tears and frustration. Anger flooded my very being, and I felt a little piece of me die. Apparently the apostle Paul had some of my thoughts because he wrote Ephesians 4:26: "Be ye angry, and sin not: let not the sun go down upon your wrath:" Looking back, my attitude seemed a bit dramatic, but drama or not, it was how I felt. I fell asleep many nights crying and woke up in the morning feeling alone, sad, mad, and angry because I didn't heed Paul's advice. Again the apostle Paul wrote Hebrews 10:23 to the spirit-filled Jews who were being persecuted, and in no way can I compare my trial to theirs, but I found comfort with his words, "Let us hold fast the profession of our faith, without wavering; (for He is faithful that promised;)" Two things I drew strength from were, He is faithful, and He promised.

In April, 1997 we began traveling for the Tupelo Children's Mansion as field representatives. After being married almost 11 years we thought perhaps we had found our family. Perhaps these were our children to love. Maybe our hearts were opening to a special kind of love. Little did we know that God had placed us in this position not just to minister to others but to be ministered to. We had no idea what God had planned for us, but we were open to anything. I enjoyed the prospect of traveling full time, and my attitude and spirit relaxed. I began focusing not so much on myself but on what I could do to help others. I remembered that long ago God had promised me something special, and after all, if He was the Giver, the gift had to be incredible.

UNHAPPY MOTHER'S DAY

At that time Tupelo Children's Mansion was affiliated with an adoption agency, and all their adoptions were handled through them, so we began mulling that in our minds. After counseling and prayer we decided to fill out the necessary papers and wait our turn for our miracle. We prayed that whether God wanted us to conceive or adopt, we would accept it. Could I love an adopted baby? I quickly answered that question with a resounding YES! I grew up with a girl who was adopted, and her parents reminded her every day of her life that the only reason they had her was because they couldn't conceive. I vowed I would never treat a child that way, and I knew in my heart that I would love my baby like crazy. The only reason he/she would be reminded they were adopted was to show the faithfulness of God. Kira Mortenson explained adoption like this: "God knew that it doesn't matter how your children get to your family. It just matters that they got there." We had a peace like we never dreamed and an excitement again about the future. This time we knew it would take a while for us to be a family, but we were prepared. Again, more advice was given about how we would now conceive because we were relaxed, but it didn't matter because it was fully in God's hands. We resumed traveling and never stopped praying for our baby wherever he/she was.

In the meantime, after we had been to several states and driven more than a few miles, we had returned to the Mansion in January for a series of meetings. Stan's sister, Ann, and her family came to visit us because that would be the closest we would be for a while. After small talk she told us that her pastor had preached about putting legs on your faith. He said if you had been praying about something for a while and wanted an answer that you should do something about it. She promptly went out in faith and bought two outfits: one for a baby girl and the other for a boy. When

Dreams And Plans

she handed them to us, what joy and confirmation we felt! We hung them in the closet, waited, and prayed. What had been by then 12 years of unbearable waiting, and sadness became excited anticipation. Our faith had been renewed, and we felt we were ready for anything. Other people had sent us prayer cloths and tokens of their faith that we put in our room also.

Bro. Marvin Walker was President of the Mansion at that time, and before we pulled our travel trailer off the property to head north to minister and represent TCM, he prayed over us. After asking God to bless our ministry and praying for safe travels, he took our hands in his and, as only he could do, sweetly petitioned Jesus to fulfill His promise in our lives with a baby. A few days after leaving Tupelo we had pulled into yet another church lot to set up our travel trailer for a series of services, and Stan's phone rang. Our hearts stood still as we heard the words we had longed for 12 1/2 years to hear. "Your baby boy is here!!!"

Finally, we were going to be a family of three. I found this beautiful, profound quote by David Platt that sums up my feelings perfectly: "It is important to realize that we adopt not because we are rescuers. No. We adopt because we are rescued."

Chapter 3

Can I Be Like Them?

UNHAPPY MOTHER'S DAY

Jesus taught that providing shelter for the shelterless, food for the hungry, and clothing for the naked are sacred acts. They are also the hallmark activities of mothering. When we do them from the right motive for those in our homes, it is as if we have done them for Christ Himself (Matt. 25:31-45).
—*Jen Wilkin*

I have always admired the strong women in the Bible. They seemed super-human though they were ordinary ladies who put their faith in an extraordinary God. Abigail, one of David's wives, risked her life defying an evil, godless husband to use her great wealth to provide for God's people. Mary Magdalene was a grateful, forgiven follower of our Lord, who never forgot where Jesus brought her from. Deborah was a female judge of Israel and a mighty warrior. She wasn't afraid of battles or heathen armies. Martha was a worker and a woman full of faith. She met her Lord outside the city limits to believe for her brother's resurrection. Rahab was a woman filled with courage, and she was obedient to a Jehovah she did not even yet know. She also risked her life to save God's men and her own people

"A strong woman is one who feels deeply and loves fiercely. Her tears flow as abundantly as her laughter. A strong woman is both soft and powerful, she is both practical and spiritual. A strong woman in her essence is a gift to the world." So says a Native American quote. These women of

Can I Be Like Them?

the Bible were all soft, yet powerful and strong and definitely a gift to our world. They taught us by example of their faith and courage. Many other godly ladies too numerous to mention also impacted their worlds and changed the course of Hebrew history. They were unique, and for that we remember them and their stories many centuries later. I want to be brave, strong, and true to my faith like my ancestors.

    My favorite ladies in the Bible are Ruth and Esther, however. Their stories speak to my heart, and I can view them as actual flesh and blood women, not just characters in a fairy tale. I love reading the books bearing their names, and I learn something new about them as well as myself each time. Ruth was strong and faithful, and she loved without asking anything in return. I'm not saying I have ever been as strong or faithful as her, but she inspires me to set aside my failings and strive to be a better woman. After suffering the devastating loss of her young husband, Mahlon, she returned with her beloved mother-in-law, Naomi, to Naomi's homeland of Bethlehem. Ruth 1:22 says, "So Naomi returned, and Ruth the Moabitess, her daughter in law with her, which returned out of the country of Moab: and they came to Bethlehem in the beginning of barley harvest." I, like Ruth, had a wonderful mother-in-law who was one of my best friends. We always had an easy relationship, and she loved me for me. We had each other's back. Ruth proved herself loyal to her mother-in-law, and caused the townspeople to remark about her faithfulness. When an entire town notices someones actions, a person has done something right. She was also a hard worker, spending many hours out in the barley fields making a living for herself and the now older Naomi. With all that said, she caught the eye of Boaz, a wealthy near-kinsman. He began providing for her and the wheels were set in motion to bear the ancestors of Jesus. I'm sure Naomi taught Ruth about her

UNHAPPY MOTHER'S DAY

Jehovah and she fell in love with Him and His ways. She was eventually rewarded for her faithfulness, and became an honored mother among Israelite women. Through long tiring days, and longer lonely nights she stayed faithful to the One who had changed her life and path.

Esther was one of the strongest, most fearless ladies I have ever read about in any book. Her given name was Hadassah, which is thought to mean "myrtle." A myrtle tree in Persia was associated with hope. If that is true, then Esther's name should have brought joy and peace throughout all Shushan. Being orphaned at a young age, she was raised by a devout uncle who taught her the ways of Jehovah and how to live a separated life even in captivity. After the disobedience of Queen Vashti of Persia, she was plucked up along with several other young women and put on display to possibly become queen of a foreign nation. I have to believe that because of her trust in Jehovah and her separated life she was chosen. After becoming the new wife of Ahasuerus, king of Persia, she faced sure death, but once again God had a plan. I like to think that she was not a super woman, but she was flesh and blood, and I'm sure she was nervous and faced fear and doubt. Haman was a real enemy, and he was determined to destroy her beloved people. Winston Churchill said, "You have enemies? Good. That means you've stood up for something in your life." After prayer and fasting, she shoved all the nervousness aside, held her head high, and approached her new husband, all the while knowing she was going against protocol and risking her life. Ultimately she helped save her beloved Jewish people from death. She became a model for all Christian ladies who aspire to be used of God. God had His hand of protection and blessing upon her. Esther 4:16 tells us, "Go, gather together all the Jews that are present in Shushan, and fast ye for me, and neither eat nor drink three days, night or day: I also and my maidens

Can I Be Like Them?

will fast likewise: and so will I go in unto the king, which is not according to the law: and if I perish, I perish." Oh, the things we should learn from Ruth and Esther each time we read their books.

Both women faced new challenges in a new season of life and handled them like pros. I'm sure there were times of insecurity and helplessness, but they knew they had responsibilities, and people were depending on them. Ruth faced a new country, while Esther faced a new role. Ruth faced stares because she was the foreigner, while Esther faced an intimidating man, Haman. I can only compare myself to these women when it comes to failures and insecurities because I have faced those same issues, with not as much success. When we first began traveling I was very shy and intimidated, which looking back, made me seem stuck up and aloof. I was not raised in church and had no clue who the 'famous' preachers and wives were, so when they were discussed I sat by quietly. I also had no idea about singers and the music business. Since that was who we interacted with the most, I kept my mouth closed so I would not appear as ignorant as I was. Those conversations made me feel intimidated, and when my husband urged me to take part I just stayed silent. Eventually I learned enough to make small contributions to each conversation, and I overcame my shyness enough to ask a few questions and learn. Life coach, Rob Liano said, "Once you embrace your value, talents, and strengths, it neutralizes when others think less of you." Also, because I didn't play the piano and sing, I felt like a failure. I was sure God could not use an ordinary girl who could hit a home run but not sing. I have also been a worrier and faithless. Each time I encountered bumps in life's road, I have wanted to run and hide myself until times became easier. In my heart I always knew that God was with me and He was faithful and just. Philippians 4:19 assured me, "But

UNHAPPY MOTHER'S DAY

my God shall supply all your need according to his riches in glory by Christ Jesus."

The question: Why do I worry or fret? The answer: Because I am human. God knows we are only flesh and blood, and He sees our weaknesses. He gave us the shining examples of these and other women in His Word to guide and shape us. He never expects us to be perfect and unafraid, He just expects us to follow I Peter 5:7, "Casting all your care upon him; for he careth for you." With a caretaker like Jesus we/you/I should never be afraid. God cared enough to come to earth and die for our souls. Why should we fret when we are not exactly what someone else is? Maybe we should look at it as if they are not who we are. Why do I always sell myself short? God made me as me, and He knows exactly what I should be doing, and if I strive to do that to the best of my ability I have no reason to hang my head. Lisa-Jo Baker encouraged, "There is nothing ordinary about you. You are a DAUGHTER OF THE KING, and your story is SIGNIFICANT." Wow, once again—we matter. I'm not the grandmother of a king, and I'm not a queen, but I'm me and I matter.

As I have said before, I sometimes forget that these were real women with real hurts and struggles. They are not just 'characters' in nice little Bible stories. They both went through things that I can't imagine. They lost loved ones and were cared for by others for a while. Both women married men who were of a different nationality and had very different customs and ways, but apparently it was what their Jehovah wanted. Both were in a foreign land and lived among strangers. While I can't fully compare myself to Ruth and Esther, I can compare myself to others who appear to have a bit more human frailties.

Can I Be Like Them?

I have been like Hannah who had to watch while she was taunted. Who wouldn't be jealous? Peninnah had what she wanted, and every day of her life Hannah felt like she flaunted it. She overcame and was blessed with a strong son. Psalm 126:5-6 says, " They that sow in tears shall reap in joy. He that goeth forth and weepeth, bearing precious seed, shall doubtless come again with rejoicing, bringing his sheaves with him." Jealousy is a terrible emotion. "Jealousy is the art of counting someone else's blessings instead of your own."

Rachel thought she had it all. Marrying her best friend, but was betrayed by a loved one and eventually her own body. She finally bore a life changer, Psalm 34:17-18 tells us, "The righteous cry, and the Lord heareth, and delivereth them out of all their troubles. The Lord is nigh unto them that are of a broken heart; and saveth such as be of a contrite spirit." Nothing in life to me hurts as much as betrayal. "Betrayal is never easy to handle and there is no right way to accept it" wrote Christine Feehan.

Sarah became anxious and tried to force God into action. The bad decision she made has had severe consequences from that time forward for the entire world. She gave birth to a mighty man of God who in turn became a father of many nations. "Hear my prayer, O Lord, give ear to my supplications; in thy faithfulness answer me, and in thy righteousness," states Psalm 143:1. Impatience with a patient God is not His will. "Impatience can cause wise people to do foolish things," penned author Janette Oke.

Two nameless, faceless women became mothers to exceptional men, but they seemed inconsequential. No name, no glory. They appeared not to matter to anyone but Jehovah.

UNHAPPY MOTHER'S DAY

Their sons however made a name for themselves. They were true Proverbs 31 women and verses 25, 28 describe them, "Strength and honor are her clothing; and she shall rejoice in time to come. Her children arise up, and call her blessed; her husband also, and he praiseth her." Sometimes anonymous people are the gasoline to the engine. Unseen but necessary. "Many of the bravest never are known, and get no praise. [But] that does not lessen their beauty..." Louisa May Alcott

Finally, Elizabeth, who was doing what God had called her to do, faced the greatest foe any woman could face. Aging. Too old to be of any use. Too old to change her circumstances, and finally, she was too old for a baby, but she produced the forerunner to our Savior. Psalm 145:21 says it like this, "My mouth shall speak the praise of the Lord; and let all flesh bless his holy name for ever and ever." Nothing can be done to stop aging, but learning to grow old gracefully is necessary. "Aging is not lost youth but a new stage of opportunity and strength," wrote Betty Friedan.

I do know the Bible says in 2 Corinthians 10:12, "For we dare not make ourselves of the number, or compare ourselves with some that commend themselves: but they measuring themselves by themselves, and comparing themselves among themselves, are not wise." We are all made up differently, and all ladies cope with things in different ways. Some use silence, while others use tears. Some fuss and fume, while others turn inward. At times I have used all these emotions to carry me through a storm. I have silently raged about the unfairness of life and questioned every woman's need for another child. God loved me enough to gently chastise me though, and He reaffirmed it in 2 Chronicles 19:7, " Wherefore now let the fear of the Lord be upon you; take heed and do it: for there is no iniquity

Can I Be Like Them?

with the Lord our God, nor respect of persons, nor taking of gifts." He didn't love me less than others, He was just teaching me things, and apparently I was a slow learner. S. C. Lourie's quote, though whimsical, is spot on, "Breathe, darling. This is just a chapter, not your whole story." Each life is full of chapters, and God is not finished with your book until we rest in sweet peace in the arms of our Lord.

I can identify with all of those women. Their hurts, fears, and struggles. I have been seemingly faithless, jealous, hateful, and bitter, but God never failed. I believe He knew my heart and understood. He never condones wrong attitudes or actions but does know that we are all too human. He loved, cleansed, and forgave me each time wrong thoughts bombarded my mind. "If we confess our sins, He is faithful and just to forgive us our sins and to cleanse us from all unrighteousness," according to I John 1:9. Deuteronomy 7:9 says, "Know therefore that the Lord thy God, He is God, the faithful God which keepeth covenant and mercy with them that love Him and keep His commandments to a thousand generations." He not only blesses us, but also our future generations.

I want to explore each of these ladies to see if I can find anything in their lives to make me a better woman and more Christ-like. What were their true feelings and beliefs? Better yet, how did they handle the obstacles placed in their way? Proverbs 13:12 says, "Hope deferred maketh the heart sick: but when the desire cometh, it is a tree of life." I found the perfect explanation of the first part of that verse in Gill's Exposition of the Entire Bible, "Hope deferred maketh the heart sick: "That is, the object hoped for; if it is not enjoyed so soon as expected, at least if it is delayed any length of time, the mind becomes uneasy, the heart sinks and fails, and the

UNHAPPY MOTHER'S DAY

man is dispirited and ready to despond, and give up all hope of enjoying the desired blessing; whether it be deliverance from any evil, or the possession of any good." This goes way beyond the longing for a child. It borders on distrust. Distrust of the One whom we should never even begin to be suspicious of. He always has our best interest at heart and will never withhold or give for that matter anything that would be our downfall. Trust Him for your family, home, livelihood, marriage, and anything else you're worried about. He knows and sees it all and will come through when you're ready and the time is right.

Were they the super women that we suppose, or did they have human faults and failings like me? The Bible says we all have faith, but it seems to be viewed differently. To some faith is treated like magic. Poof, and the problems are supposed to dissipate. Perhaps some tried to strong-arm God. If He withheld from them they would withhold their praise and worship too. Or, maybe some trials are just too much for some ladies. Eventually though, all the women of old came around to believing and trusting that He would do the right thing for the right reason. When it was time, their promised child would be born. Corrie Ten Boom said it like this, "Faith sees the invisible, believes the unbelievable, and receives the impossible. Elizabeth Elliot wrote, "The God who created names, and numbers the stars in the heavens also numbers the hairs of my head. He pays attention to very big things and to very small ones. What matters to me matters to Him, and that changes my life." Is there anything in these women that I can see and let it change my life? Psalm 25:4-5 says, "Shew me thy ways, O Lord; teach me thy paths, Lead me in thy truth, and teach me: for thou art the God of my salvation; on thee do I wait all the day." These beautiful women were made to wait just like me, but they were teachable, and He changed their lives

Can I Be Like Them?

along with a nation which changed an entire world. Let me learn to wait on you, Lord, and teach me through them. Help me to be strong, and change my part of the world. The author Jonathan Harnish said, "The strongest people are not those who show strength in front of the world, but those who fight and win battles that others do not know anything about."

Chapter 4

Don't Be Jealous, Hannah

UNHAPPY MOTHER'S DAY

Only God Himself fully appreciates the influence of a Christian mother in the molding of character in her children.
—Billy Graham

Romans 12:15 tells us, "Rejoice with them that do rejoice, and weep with them that weep". There are two verbs in that verse that we have to contend with: rejoicing and weeping. One is a much easier task than the other. Rejoice is: feel or show great joy or delight. Weep is: to express deep sorrow. I have been over the moon with joy for a friend's accomplishments, but I have also been in the depths of despair for another's loss.

Rejoice-

I have heard that particular verse preached over and over my whole Christian life, and I have tried to live by that rule. Sometimes without much success. When a friend got a raise or a new car I have been truly happy: if I thought they needed it. If someone received a job promotion I rejoiced: if I thought they needed it. That new house they bought? I rejoiced. If I thought they needed it. But when I was sure they didn't deserve or need it I went into full fledged pouting mode. I was the judge and jury. I'm not sure when I took over our great God's job, but I did. I weighed every situation and made sure they were all equal and fair. I honestly would rejoice with my whole heart, but I'm not sure I 'showed great joy or delight' as the Bible instructs. I had to make sure they required and/or warranted it.

Don't Be Jealous, Hannah

There were times when we were first married that there was more month at the end of the money, and I honestly struggled watching some of my friends buy what I considered frivolous items. I imagined I could've spent that same amount and paid off a bill. I am only now realizing that it was none of my business what they purchased or how much they paid. God overlooked my attitude and provided all our needs. The Canadian poet Margaret Atwood summed up my feelings of jealousy like this, "You can only be jealous of someone who has something you think you ought to have yourself." Pretty basic but absolutely true.

Weep-

Now, weeping is another story. I feel as if I have always been tender hearted toward those in need. My heart truly ached for people who lost things, loved ones, or possessions. When we lived in Kennett, Missouri, our neighbor's house burned down, and I was one of the first people over with food and clothing. It wasn't much, but it was what I could do. One day while we were traveling for the Tupelo Children's Mansion, my husband and I were going somewhere on a time schedule and didn't have long to eat, so we decided on a fast food drive through. I griped the whole time until we pulled up and saw a man rifling in the trash for his meal. I'm telling you that hamburger stuck in my throat, and that is a show and tell lesson I will never forget. God has a way of driving a point home, and that point was to always be thankful no matter what. By the way, Stan gave the man money, and we watched his step become lighter as he headed in to order a proper meal. I'm not patting myself on the back, but I cry for people who have suffered loss. My heart is touched when people lose things important to them, but do I express deep sorrow?

UNHAPPY MOTHER'S DAY

It is hard to explain loss. Most times loss is tragic, but sometimes it can be a blessing in disguise. Sometimes the first thing I think is utter devastation and complete ruin, but that is not always the case. The Roman philosopher Marcus Aurelius sums it up well, "Loss is nothing else but change, and change is Nature's delight." Without change there would be no growth, and without loss we would never realize how blessed we actually are. After a forest fire the trees grow back. It is a slow process, but regeneration takes place. Nevertheless, weeping with people is sure a whole lot easier than rejoicing with them. Weeping requires heart felt, sometimes gut wrenching emotions, while rejoicing requires condemnation and judging, so I thought. I realize now that jealousy gave me a warped sense of perception.

Have you ever wanted something so desperately that you could almost taste it? It drove you, and it was all you could do to function. You just could not stop meditating on it, and day after day it consumed you. You could not think straight, and it made you jealous to the point of alienating friends who had what you desired. I was that way about wanting a child. I felt that I needed what they needed, but more, and I was certainly more than worthy of it. It didn't matter if they ever got it or not. I had a horrible attitude at times, but God was merciful. I felt that it just wasn't fair. Every new baby in the family or at church seemed a slap in the face. I would grieve over every pregnancy story. I felt my heart would burst with sadness. Now, it sounds so dramatic, but at the time it was almost a debilitating sorrow. The last half of Psalm 30:5 says, "Weeping may endure for a night, but joy cometh in the morning." The night seemed a never-ending blackness, and I feared that the beautiful, joyful morning the Psalmist wrote about would never come.

Don't Be Jealous, Hannah

Hannah, one of the two wives of Elkanah, may have been like that. She wanted a child so desperately that I imagine it consumed her just like it did me. Each story in the Bible was recorded for a purpose, and Hannah's profound emotions were written perfectly. I Samuel 2:10 says, "And she was in bitterness of soul, and she prayed unto the Lord, and wept sore." She watched every day while her nemesis, Peninnah, who appeared to bear children so easily, seemed to gloat over her babies. It is thought that Elkanah took Peninnah to wife only because of Hannah's barrenness. Because he was a Levite he took his responsibility to carry on the lineage very seriously. Having sons were as important to a Jewish man as breathing air. After realizing that Hannah wasn't going to bear a son, Elkanah couldn't let his lineage stop. Hannah, I'm sure, realized this, and that made her situation even more dire. She seemed a complete and utter failure. Hannah felt that Peninnah gave Elkanah what she couldn't; therefore, although Hannah was first choice, she felt second rate.

Jealousy makes a person's mind think crazy thoughts: thoughts a Christian woman should never entertain. Thoughts like, "She can't even control those kids," or " I could raise them so much better," or "She doesn't even deserve her children," and "I've been way more faithful than her." I'm wondering if Hannah thought, "Peninnah wasn't his first choice but is acting like someone special." I know I probably would have. Those are dangerous thoughts because a person cannot, and best not, judge someone else's actions, walk with God, or consecration to Him. Peninnah couldn't help her fruitfulness anymore than Hannah her barrenness.

Author Shannon L. Alder summed up jealousy this way, "Insecure people only eclipse your sun because they're

UNHAPPY MOTHER'S DAY

jealous of your daylight and tired of their dark, starless nights." Because Joseph was his father's favorite son it caused friction and jealousy with his older brothers. What on earth would cause rational men to dream up such an irrational and devious plan on their own flesh and blood? Jealousy. Plain and simple. Little did they know that God used their wickedness to fulfill His great plan. Through their maliciousness God showed himself strong. Esau was another man whom jealousy consumed. He was jealous of Jacob's birthright, a blessing that he was beaten out of, and he vowed to kill Jacob as soon as their father died. But God used that to build a great nation. God knew the jealous hearts of Joseph's brothers, and Esau, but He used it to His advantage. They would probably have been angry to know their evil thoughts were guided by a pure, holy Savior. Hebrews 4:12 tells us Who the true Judge is: "For the word of God is quick, and powerful, and sharper than any twoedged sword, piercing even to the dividing asunder of soul and spirit, and of the joints and marrow, and is a discerner of the thoughts and intents of the heart." I should have known to leave the judging to Him, but sometimes it takes me a while. I am so thankful that my loving Lord knows the deep down intents of my heart.

    I know a thing or two about jealousy because at one time or another for 12 1/2 years those were my thoughts. I was a Hannah. No, Stan didn't take another wife and never gave me reason to be jealous of him, but still I felt I couldn't control those feelings. What good was I as a minister's wife? I couldn't sing or play the piano, so that automatically disqualified me to be a preacher's wife and used of God. Now because I couldn't give him a baby, the cute little, perfect preachers' family apparently wasn't meant to be either. There you have it: I was a complete failure. Jealousy can't see inside you and unfortunately doesn't care

Don't Be Jealous, Hannah

that you're destroying your soul. Jealousy was eating at me. I craved just one baby. I felt that I wasn't asking much. Some of the women who were much younger than I were expecting their second or third baby, and sometimes it was all I could do to be civil. I tried to politely ignore anyone with a baby. I would hold and play with one to avoid being rude, but as I took in the feel and smell of a little one, I felt as if another knife was plunging into my heart. I did and said all the right things and smiled on the outside, but inside I was a mess of terribly ugly and angry emotions.

I'm sure when Hannah watched Elkanah interact with his children from Penninah that she was even more grieved. Such a happy sight was marred by jealousy. "How dare he be happy," she may have mused. Hannah was so upset that she couldn't eat and cried fervently, according to the Bible. Elkanah loved her so much, but he couldn't understand her grief, for after all, she was his chosen love. He loved her for her and not for what she could give him. He knew she wanted a son desperately but thought that his love for her could compensate for her barrenness. In I Samuel 1:8 Elkanah asks Hannah, "Am I not better to thee than ten sons?" He just didn't get it. A supportive husband's love means the world, but nothing compares to the feeling of being a complete family. Holding and loving your very own baby is joy beyond compare. I knew Stan was there for me and always would be, but I felt I would never be whole and be useful unless I had a baby. God had ordained us as a couple, but I couldn't see that Stan loved me no matter what. His love never diminished and seemingly grew with each passing year. Sometimes I wondered if it would, but deep in my heart I knew he would never quit loving me, no matter my shortcomings.

UNHAPPY MOTHER'S DAY

I Samuel 1:6 states that Hannah's adversary, "Also provoked her sore." Nothing hurts more than being made fun of, especially for something that you can't help. I have seen the sad faces of children who have been ridiculed or mocked for an impediment. There is no sadder sight. Real or imagined, I felt every mother I interacted with was provoking me. Even the sweetest of ladies I saw as mocking. Sometimes I didn't see a kind, friendly smile; rather, I saw a condescending smirk. If a group of women were chatting, I felt as if they were talking about me. Jealousy really gives a person a feeling of self-importance. What would make me think everything was about me and everyone was talking about me? If jealousy takes root it can and will alienate you from those who love and care the most for you. I had some of the most fantastic friends and family who I know prayed for me on a daily basis, but that just wasn't enough. Now I know how blessed I was, but then I was clouded by jealousy. Hannah's problem was not Peninah or Elkanah, it was with herself. She had to deal with feelings of inadequacy and deficiency. Just like me. I was a Hannah to a T.

It actually wasn't her body that was the problem at all. It was the Lord who had "shut up her womb." It was His will, and everything would work out. God's plans are amazing if we will submit to His will and wait patiently. "Wait on the Lord: be of good courage, and he shall strengthen thine heart: wait, I say, on the Lord" (Psalm 27:14). Once I had surrendered my will and prayed completely through, I realized my problem was not God. It was simply me. It didn't happen in the first prayer meeting but was a process. Every doctor I consulted with saw no reason for my infertility and even suggested that sometimes it is possibly the husband's issue. We never got tested but just trusted God. Finally, it was determined I needed a hysterectomy. In the pre-op for my hysterectomy, the doctor told me my womb was tilted

Don't Be Jealous, Hannah

and I would probably never have been able to conceive a baby. Little did he know. Our God can do anything even bypass a womb issue.

Hannah lived a life of prayer and consecration. She was also faithful to church. She went to the synagogue yearly with her husband as he offered sacrifices for his family. You could say she was a perfect Christian wife, but every time she saw Peninah, something changed a little bit. The facade of perfection faded, and the Bible says she began to fret. Other words for fret are: fume, worry, and rage. None of those feelings are of God, and if not prayed through will destroy a person. When a person is fretting, they are not trusting God. I know for a fact that those ugly feelings will get you in trouble. So many innocent friends I smarted off to were left bewildered by my actions. Later, I apologized but was too ashamed to reveal the source of my anger. I blamed it on stress or fatigue. I couldn't admit to everyone that I was a tangle of hateful feelings. I had to appear a poised and perfect preachers wife, when actually I was a jealous mess. Sharon Alder said, "Anger, resentment and jealousy doesn't change the heart of others—it only changes yours." I needed to be changed for sure, but not that way.

Elkanah was a prime example of a proper Jewish husband. He led his family in temple worship every year. What greater example of a loving, godly husband than to lead your family in prayer and praise. Proverbs 22:6 says, "Train up a child in the way he should go and when he is old, he will not depart from it." Elkanah was living that verse to lead and guide his wives and children. Hannah followed his lead but for a different reason. She knew that Jehovah was her only answer, and the temple was the place to receive it.

UNHAPPY MOTHER'S DAY

> And she was in bitterness of soul, and prayed unto the Lord, and wept sore. And she vowed a vow, and said, O Lord of hosts, if thou wilt indeed look on the affliction of thine handmaid, and remember me, and not forget thine handmaid, but wilt give unto thine handmaid a man child, then I will give him unto the Lord all the days of his life, and there shall no razor come upon his head.
>
> I Samuel 1:10-11

She was in so much anguish that she caught the attention of Eli the priest, and he proclaimed in verse 17, "Then Eli answered and said, Go in peace: and the God of Israel grant thee thy petition that thou hast asked of him." I was again like Hannah. I had prayed and cried until there were no more tears or words. My mouth just couldn't express what my heart felt. I, too, was in "bitterness of soul." The soul is described as the core of your being. Hannah and I were in pain to the very core of our existence.

"Go in peace." Had she heard Eli correctly? Was it truly going to happen? Had Jehovah answered her prayer? Hannah was going to be a mother at last. I believe more than anything she felt a sweet, divine peace. Finally, the thing that had eluded her for years, the thing she had been mocked and teased about and berated and brow beaten for was coming to pass. She was going to be a mother, and nothing could wipe the smile off her face. She left the synagogue with more peace than she ever imagined. No more anguish. No more tears or ugly hateful feelings. Just complete peace and a joy

Don't Be Jealous, Hannah

that she felt deep in her very soul. She watched Peninnah's children differently now with joy and anticipation. Before Hannah conceived, the first part of verse 19 says, "And they rose up in the morning early, and worshipped before the LORD...." Worship preceded conception!

I remember when we finally decided to fill out the papers for adoption. I had asked myself some pretty tough questions about it. Could I honestly love an adopted baby and care for it as my own? I had family who was adopted, and I loved them because they were my family. I knew deep down in my soul that if God trusted us with a little one it would be my 'own.' We felt God's blessing and knew that now anything was possible. We could still bear a child even though the papers were complete, but our hearts were open for anything. Finally, sweet peace. It was going to happen in God's perfect time. I felt totally relaxed just knowing that I had finally given my longing and desire to God.

When our "Samuel" was given to us of the Lord, my heart was overwhelmed with emotion: joy, excitement, and a little fear. Would I be the mother that he needed? Would I raise him to live for the Lord? Would he love me as much as I loved him? There was no way for me to know all the answers to those questions, so I determined to do as Hannah had done. According to I Samuel 1:27-28 Hannah said, "For this child I prayed; and the Lord hath given me my petition which I asked of him: Therefore also I have lent him to the Lord; as long as he liveth he shall be lent to the Lord. And he worshipped the Lord there." Eli was happy for her and gave her his blessing, by worshiping the Lord with her. My sister-in-law, Ann, had bought us a picture with that very verse on it. Talk about confirmation!

UNHAPPY MOTHER'S DAY

Stan and I did as Hannah but not quite to her extreme. We 'lent him to the Lord' when he was a few weeks old in front of friends and family. Our pastor, Brother McGruder, knew of our struggle and rejoiced with us along with our dear parents and siblings. Everyone praised the Lord for answering our heartfelt prayer. Samuel was in a sense adopted by Eli and grew up in a preacher's home and became a mighty man. A leader of his people. We could only hope and pray that our son would do the same, but with God's hand on him, he was destined for great things. Hannah and I followed Psalm 96:8, "Give unto the Lord the glory due unto his name: bring an offering, and come into his courts." An offering is "something offered in worship or devotion." (dictionary.com) Benjamin was our offering to our wonderful, miracle working Savior.

When I finally gave God my jealousy and anger He changed my heart. I felt as if a weight had been lifted, and I could see things better. The world was brighter, clearer, and sharper. I should have known all the time that my friends weren't mocking me and God wasn't against me. When we filled out the adoption papers we still didn't have a baby just yet, but I knew deep in my heart that He knew what was best for me. In His perfect time, all would be made right. A quote from a hymn written by William Cowper sums it all up, "God moves in mysterious ways; His wonders to perform; He plans His footsteps in the sea, and rides upon the storm." If I know anything about my God, it's that He is an amazing storm rider. He can do anything if we just give Him the problem. Psalm 119:165 sums it up perfectly, "Great peace have they which love thy law and nothing shall offend them." Peace, great peace. He is the Peace Speaker. Let Him calm your storm of jealous emotions and there will be smoother sailing in your family and life.

Don't Be Jealous, Hannah

> Behold, I go forward, but he is not there; and backward, but I cannot perceive him: On the left hand, where he doth work, but I cannot behold him: he hideth himself on the right hand, that I cannot see him: But he knoweth the way that I take: when he hath tried me, I shall come forth as gold.
>
> Job 23:8-10

Believe me, I lived every feeling of these verses every day of those 12 years. But when verse 10 arrived with the words, "he knoweth the way that I take" and "I shall come forth as gold," my soul thundered, and I felt as if an angel was lightening my load, and I was rejuvenated. God's words always have a way of making things better if we would read and obey! A friend posted this from the radio station 95.1shinefm, "Complaining about a silent God while your Bible is closed, is like complaining about not getting texts when your phone is turned off." I found this poem by an anonymous source that sums up my feelings about my Benjamin,

> *You are the poem*
> *I dreamed of writing.*
> *The masterpiece*
> *I longed to paint...*
> *You are the shining star*
> *I reached for*
> *In my ever hopeful quest*
> *for life fulfilled...*
> *You are my child*
> *Now with all things*
> *I AM BLESSED.*

UNHAPPY MOTHER'S DAY

God can do absolutely anything you ask, but it may not be in your time. He knows what we need, when we need it. Don't be judgmental and jealous over others accomplishments. If you're faithful He will provide. Don't give up on that healing, job, home and family. In His perfect time, my friend, He will provide.

Chapter 5

Rachel, It's Not Your Fault

UNHAPPY MOTHER'S DAY

Your greatest contribution to the kingdom of God might not be something you do, but someone you raise.
—Andy Stanley

Trust. What a reassuring word, yet what a frightening emotion. That word gives me an odd, precarious feeling sometimes. According to the Merriam-Webster dictionary, trust is: "a firm belief in the character, strength, or truth of someone or something." Trust is easy when we are young children and don't have to worry about the next step, but it becomes more difficult as a person ages and realizes that every move has consequences. At times people have a way of letting you down: most often without even meaning to, and sometimes the betrayal is not real but only in your mind. As a child you automatically trust and jump in daddy's arms from the sofa or a chair without giving a thought to danger. Kids should always know that the adults in their lives are going to be there and take care of them. But adults have second thoughts about trusting and taking chances on people or things. Time and life have taken a toll on some people, and without really knowing or trusting God, we tend to guard ourselves and make sure not to let anyone in who would hurt us or let us down. Risks are a scary proposition. You risk job changes, family changes, church changes, or location changes, and all these are frightening. Over your entire life, what will you face? Those changes may and often can lead to heartache if you don't trust in the One who never fails. You quickly become jaded, and if you're not careful trust is replaced with cynicism. Cynicism then leads to worry and

Rachel, It's Not Your Fault

disorder in your spirit. Olympic champion Allyson Felix puts trust this way: "The most important lesson that I have learned is to trust God in every circumstance. Lots of times we go through different trials and following God's plan seems like it doesn't make any sense at all. God is always in control and he will never leave us." I have been to the point where I was let down and afraid to trust again, and I had every bit of peace sucked out of my life. It is terribly hard to go forward when you're always looking back with hurt and anger, but His word says in Numbers 6:26, "The Lord lift up his countenance upon thee, and give thee peace." My husband always says, "Faith is believing God can do anything. Trust is believing God to do the right thing for my life."

The story of Rachel and Jacob is one of my favorites. It is romantic and idyllic, and when reading it, my mind goes a thousand different places. They were a beautiful couple who had great possibilities for their future because God had divinely put them together and ordained their destiny just like me and Stan. God couldn't have taken two different people and put them together any more than He did us. He was a southerner through and through, and I a born and bred northern girl. He was raised in church, and I didn't get the Holy Ghost until I was 14. He listened to and sang southern gospel music, and I was contemporary to the core. He cheered for the Cardinals baseball team, and I was a Tigers fan, but love is amazing, and we meshed into a south-north couple. We listened to both styles and rooted for each other's teams. Instead of always having a civil war, we learned to wear gray and blue beautifully. It is amazing what love and God can do.

After Jacob deceived his father, Isaac, and received

UNHAPPY MOTHER'S DAY

a blessing, he was sent to his Uncle Laban's house for protection from his brother Esau. Esau became enraged after Jacob had tricked their father and stolen his birthright. He vowed to get revenge and kill Jacob when their father was dead. It was at Laban's house that Jacob found refuge and the love of his life, Rachel. God always has a way of finding 'that person' for you if you trust and believe and if it is ultimately His perfect will.

True love has a way of changing a person, but even after Jacob met Rachel, he was still crafty and somewhat deceitful, but a softer, more forgiving side began emerging. It was not until he came face to face with the angel that his life was completely revolutionized and changed. He was so enamored with Rachel that he was willing to do anything to gain her hand, to the point that he gave her father seven years of his life just to have her as his bride. Genesis 29:20 says, "And Jacob served seven years for Rachel; and they seemed unto him but a few days, for the love he had for her." Wow, what a story of true love and commitment! He saw her for what she was: a beautiful woman who had a servants heart. She tended her father's sheep. What if she hadn't been so faithful to her father? What if she had made an excuse not to water her father's flocks? What if Leah had been at the well that day? Rachel's story would have been so different, but she had been faithful to Laban and his instruction. God was going to unfold a beautiful story, and the nation of Israel would have a miraculous beginning.

Rachel overheard her father tell Jacob that he could marry her after his years of service were fulfilled, so all she had to do was wait and plan. What an exciting time when you know you have found 'the one' and wedding bells would soon be ringing. Imagine having seven years to plan a

Rachel, It's Not Your Fault

wedding and the funds to do anything you desire. Stan and I had 3 months and a limited budget, but we had a wonderful wedding nevertheless. What a celebration Rachel was planning. A true fairytale wedding with hopefully the 'and they lived happily ever after' ending. When the day finally arrived and the preparations were finished, Rachel knew that Jacob was waiting for her with anticipation, but what she faced was heartbreak. I have always wondered where Rachel was in all this. Did she not wonder why she wasn't being prepared for marriage according to the traditional customs, or did Laban's deception go so deep as to let her be prepared also? The Bible doesn't mention how Rachel and Leah got along before all the deceit, nor how each of them would have reacted had they known they were both being prepared for marriage. Any way it happened, her father had not only broken her heart but also her trust. To put it simply, he betrayed her. It wasn't enough that he had committed the ultimate betrayal, but he had shattered her heart in a million pieces. How could a father have done that? He knew the rules about the oldest daughter from the beginning, and he knew that he couldn't or wouldn't give away Rachel first. Was he so desperate for a laborer that he was willing to destroy his youngest daughter's trust in him? Rachel knew that she and Jacob were God-blessed and meant to be together, but now how would that ever be? Perhaps Rachel knew of Jacob's deception in the matter of his brother and figured it caught up to him. Maybe there was too much deception all the way around and they would never be together. I imagine that her faith was shaken with everyone and everything around her. Though Jacob's trickery concerning his brother wasn't her fault, she felt she had been deceived again. The old saying, "What goes around, comes around" seems to fit here. Jacob stole Esau's birthright, Leah stole his first love, and Rachel felt punished by both.

UNHAPPY MOTHER'S DAY

Don't forget Leah, though. Maybe she thought Jacob had changed his mind and she really was the chosen. Imagine her horror to discover she was still second choice and would always be. That somewhat explains her behavior toward Rachel after her children were born. She would bear children and force Jacob to love her more. Because Laban deceived her also, and arranged a loveless marriage, she was stuck forever being number two instead of letting God work and allowing her to find her true love also. In my opinion, Laban was a bad man, but God used his deception regarding his daughters to begin something magnificent. Remember, God can use anyone to do anything. He used a donkey to speak to a prophet.

When Stan and I first began talking marriage, we were both very analytical and spent hours at one of our favorite restaurants drinking soda and talking. We knew we loved each other and felt certain that God had ordained us to be together, but we also had a practical side. Could we make it on our salaries? At the time he worked for a small town radio station and I for a pediatrician in Louisiana, but I would move to Kennett and not have a job for a while. We were smart enough to know that you couldn't live on love for very long!

We asked questions about everything we could think of: health, family histories, backgrounds and future dreams, and we were open with each other because we only wanted what God wanted, but we also knew we had to be honest with each other. I remember one time in particular that Stan asked seemingly a logical question that I never hesitated a minute answering: "Would you tell me if you couldn't have children?" Well, of course I would, and never gave it another thought because the question was absurd. Everyone that

Rachel, It's Not Your Fault

wanted to could have children, so I thought. I was always healthy and active and never had any problems. He was a 'baby magnet' and we both knew we wanted kids. Several years down our childless journey, I thought about that question many times, and I was racked with guilt. I honestly didn't know at the time I would struggle with infertility, but nonetheless, I felt I had deceived him. Did he feel the same? One night in a fit of hopeless tears I asked him, and he gently and lovingly assured me that it had never crossed his mind. He said he didn't even remember asking me that question. I wanted to believe him, but every month thereafter I had the same nagging question. Was I a deceiver? Did perhaps my subconscious know what my body didn't?

Jacob did what any good Hebrew man would do and accepted Leah as his wife, but he loved Rachel so much that he served seven more years just for her hand in marriage. Polygamy wasn't a big deal back then, and was accepted by the Jewish people. Because she knew how much he cared for her and that they were meant to be together, she must have been thrilled and began her wedding plans once again. Jacob and Rachel were wary though, because Laban had made it a habit of betraying the young couple. What would Laban try to pull now? First with the daughters and then eventually with the animals. They had no faith in him at all. Once they were deceived, it was hard to trust him, but finally after they were married they had enough of Laban and his lies so much so that they left Paddan-aram with the entire family in tow. Jacob, Rachel, Leah, the two maid servants, and all the children headed out on a new adventure in a new land.

Laban wasn't the only thing that had betrayed Rachel. This time it seemed that her story book life wasn't going to

UNHAPPY MOTHER'S DAY

be so rosy. She, like me, had her dream man, but the children part was proving a bit more difficult. Her very own body was betraying her. Leah had no problem conceiving, and she wasn't even the favored wife. Jacob felt a duty to Leah because he knew that she knew she wasn't his first choice, but he was in love with Rachel. Leah had to be heartbroken because she wasn't loved, but she had consolation in her sons. Genesis 29:31 states, "And when the Lord saw that Leah was hated, he opened her womb: but Rachel was barren." What is the matter with my body? Rachel must have mused. She was "beautiful and well favored" the Bible says, but that was doing her no good now. Having children with the man you love, the man of your dreams should be easy and beautiful. All it takes is a perfectly healthy woman, and Rachel thought she was. Dr. Carista Luminare-Rosen put it this way, "Parenting begins the moment you make any conscious effort to care for your own health in preparation for enhancing your child's conception." Rachel became angry and envious and blamed Jacob for her barrenness. Perhaps she felt as if Jacob, through no fault of his own, had betrayed her also. After all, he already had children with Leah. He seemed perfectly content to her. When a person is in pain they can rationalize anything. That was nonsense she knew, but it was easier to blame him than her own body. Genesis 30:1 records her angry words, "Give me children, or else I die," and he responded in the next verse, "Am I in God's stead who hath withheld from thee the fruit of the womb?" (Genesis 30:2). That had to sting for both of them. He said that God withheld a baby from her. Ouch.

When Stan and I were about seven years into our journey I became just like Rachel: envious, jealous, and felt betrayed. Secretly, I guess I blamed Stan and everything around me. The doctors didn't find anything physically wrong, and it was before my autoimmune issues were

Rachel, It's Not Your Fault

discovered, so it had to be other outside factors. My mind said, Stan traveled a lot, so it must never have been the right time. I blamed him and the singing group. "If he would just stay home we could have a family like all our friends," I griped. We really didn't have the finances to support a child. I worked two jobs, so I would have to either quit or have babysitters. I blamed the jobs. But the biggest lie my head told me was, Stan probably didn't even want a baby. At least not as much as I did. I saw him playing with the kids at church and ridiculously assumed that they replaced his own desire for a baby. He has never been the whining type, so other than telling me he wanted a child, I had no proof. After all, I felt the weight of the world on my shoulders each month and thought everyone who looked at me could see the invisible sign: hey, world, she's childless. I thought anyone could see that Stan didn't have a care in the world (so I thought) and never thought about one day dreaming he would bear the title, daddy. That couldn't have been further from the truth. He was a private person, and didn't want to add to my hurt by sharing his pain with me. I never really saw the way he longingly looked at babies at church and held them every chance he got. To this day he is "Uncle Stan" to many grown kids. He longed for a baby as much as I, but I was so self absorbed that I couldn't see that. Author Stephen Kendrick says, "Almost every sinful action ever committed can be traced back to a selfish motive. It is a trait we hate in other people but justify in ourselves." I was selfish and either didn't know or care most of the time. His heart ached just like mine, but I was more vocal about it.

The plain and simple fact was that I had been betrayed just like Rachel. I had parents who loved me beyond question, so it wasn't them. My husband was my best friend and loved and protected me, and would give his life for me, so it wasn't him. It wasn't even the circumstances around

UNHAPPY MOTHER'S DAY

me. It was ME. My aggravating, uncooperative body was betraying me month after upsetting month. I was still just as active and healthy as ever, and I trusted it to work right, but it just wouldn't do it's job.

I cried, "God, I really don't understand this." Like Rachel and Jacob, I knew we were meant to be together and knew deep in my soul that somehow, someway we were meant to have a child. God, I prayed, "Your servants prophesied that we would have a son. How long, Lord? Have you forgotten?" What I needed was in Philippians 4:6-7, "Be careful for nothing; but in every thing by prayer and supplication with thanksgiving let your requests be made known unto God. And the peace of God, which passeth all understanding, shall keep your hearts and minds through Christ Jesus." I implored God everyday for a baby, but with no luck. But was I doing it properly? As I examine that scripture, one huge word jumps off the page to me: with THANKSGIVING! When I was at my lowest during prayer, I can't remember pleading with thanksgiving. Usually I was feeling sorry for myself and being jealous of others. But God promises peace after thanksgiving, and I eventually found that peace. The 18th century theologian Albert Barnes said, "We can always find something to be thankful for, and there may be reasons why we ought to be thankful for even those dispensations which appear dark and frowning." Bodies can be stubborn and let us down, but God is never that way. Jim Cymbala said it like this: "Faith deals with the invisible things of God. It refuses to be ruled by the physical senses. Faith is able to say, 'You can do what you like, because I know God is going to take care of me. He has promised to bless me where he leads me.' Remember that even when every demon in hell stands against us, the God of Abraham remains faithful to all his promises. Jesus Christ can do anything but fail his own people who trust him."

Rachel, It's Not Your Fault

Finally, year after painful year of watching Leah and the two handmaids Billah and Zilpah conceive and bear Jacob children, it was Rachel's turn. Genesis 30:22-23 states it beautifully: "And God remembered Rachel, and hearkened to her, and opened her womb And she conceived, and bare a son, and said God hath taken away my reproach." He remembered her! I love that phrase because, in order to remember something, you have to have known about it previously and just tucked it away for later. God has always known where she was and she wasn't betrayed after all. It just hadn't been God's time. After nine, beautiful and suspenseful months, she named her firstborn child, Joseph, and he was destined for greatness. It may have taken a while, but oh how sweet and wonderful it was!

Then when it seemed I couldn't trust anymore, our "Joseph" finally arrived. God remembered me, and all the pain and hurt disappeared. I realized that the only betrayal was in my mind. God had never betrayed me. He had a plan and He stuck with it. Through all of my whining and complaining, God never strayed from His course and best of all never judged me. He understood all of my hurt and grief. He knew that I didn't mean the hateful things I had said in my heart. Even when my body wouldn't cooperate, I see now that He had bigger and much grander plans. God always works on both ends of the problem. There was a "Joseph" needing us just as much as we needed him. God's ways are not our ways, and His timing is always perfect. God surely blessed us with our little man, and Psalm 40:4 was right when it said, " Blessed is the man that maketh Jehovah his trust." Through the years I did trust Him. Sometimes it was pretty weak, but it was still trust. Though month after month my body was anything but reliable, God was ever so faithful. In my unrighteousness, He was righteous. In my chaos, He was peace, and in my failings, He was always steadfast. One

UNHAPPY MOTHER'S DAY

of the sweetest quotes that I have ever read is this one from Shel Silverstein, and it says it exactly how I feel about my Benji, "And she loved a (not so) little boy very, very much, even more than she loved herself."

If you're feeling betrayed right now, forget about outside circumstances and people. Don't listen to the troubling thoughts in your mind. God will never betray you. Never give up hope, because what God promises He will bring it to pass, and it will be a beautiful, perfect thing. God knows exactly what you need when you need it. Romans 11:33 reads, "O the depth of the riches both of the wisdom and knowledge of God! how unsearchable are his judgments, and his ways past finding out!" Psalm 37:34 says, "Wait on the Lord, and keep his way and he shall exalt thee." There is nothing like having your family right in the center of God's will knowing that you waited on His perfect time. Every time I look into my boy's face I see God's perfect plan being played out again. Never, ever forget that God and His word is the only trustworthy source for our families. Trust Him with your body. Trust Him with your circumstances, but most of all, trust Him with your family.

"Never be afraid to trust an unknown future to a known God." Only a woman who had been through what Corrie Ten Boom had could write this beautiful quote on trust. She lived a life of trust because at times that is all she could do. Let us all be Corrie's.

Our minds play an important role in not only our mental health but also our physical health. I have found that the days I wake up in a bad mood, everything around me is ugly and upsetting, but on the good days all seems sunshine and roses. This beautiful thought by Brittney Moses has

Rachel, It's Not Your Fault

uplifted my spirits many times:

> *"When it feels like you're empty and hurting alone,*
> *know that God is present in this space with you.*
> *And as you draw near to Him,*
> *He will draw near to you.*
> *He sees what no one sees,*
> *He hears what isn't said*
> *but is cried out by the heart*
> *and He will restore you."*

What are you facing right now? Do you feel alone, forsaken and completely empty? Are your troubles piling up into an impossible mound of hopelessness. Maybe today is a 'sunny' day, but you've been here before and know that tomorrow you could be enveloped in an angry cloud of darkness like days before. Are you waiting for the 'other shoe to fall?' Think about it. Has God led you this far? Remember the story of the children of Israel being led out of Egypt. I'm sure they were nervous about their future but also excited about God's promised land. They were ready to hurry and get there, set up housekeeping, and begin building their new nation, but what was God doing making them take a longer way.

> And it came to pass, when Pharaoh had let the people go, that God led them not by the way of the land of the Philistines, although that was near; for God said, Lest peradventure the people repent when they see war, and they return to Egypt: but God led the people about, by the way of the wilderness by the Red Sea: and the children of Israel went up armed out of the land of Egypt.
>
> Exodus 13:17-18

UNHAPPY MOTHER'S DAY

They were anxious and in a hurry, but their Jehovah knew best. When we get anxious and frustrated about God taking His sweet time, remember that He sees the entire journey we're on and knows what roads we should take to get us there safely and effectively. Trust Him! Trust Him! Trust HIM!

Chapter 6

Wait For It, Sarah

UNHAPPY MOTHER'S DAY

I remember my mother's prayers and they have always followed me. They have clung to me all my life.
—*Abraham Lincoln*

Let's talk about a word called confidence. Do you have confidence? Do I? I have all the confidence in the world in my God and His ability to keep me, but sometimes I have absolutely none in myself. Growing up, I was pretty fearless on the baseball field and basketball court, but put me in front of a crowd to speak or sing and I forget the words. No confidence. I know many preachers and singers who appear as if they have all the confidence in the world, but found out later that they were unsure of themselves. They exuded confidence because of their trust in the Lord. They left everything to Him and gave God their ministry and talents to use as He saw fit. My mentor and pastor's wife, Sister Priscilla McGruder, was a great example. I thought she walked on water and never got nervous or rattled because she was the epitome of poise or courage. She always seemed confident. It was years later that I learned that for years she stood in front of the microphone to sing and held on and rarely looked up. Wow! Who would have ever thought that that powerhouse of a godly woman lacked confidence?

I view the inventor Thomas Edison to be a very confident and successful person, but was he truly? He said himself, "I have not failed, I've just found 10,000 ways that won't work." So, obviously he didn't succeed 100% of the time, but he was confident in his abilities and never gave up.

Wait For It, Sarah

Three things confident people do are: don't fear self doubt, don't fear failure, and the most important I believe is, don't confuse confidence with arrogance.

One definition of confidence is: a feeling or belief that you can do something well or succeed at something or the feeling of being certain that something will happen or that something is true. A different definition that struck a chord in my soul was a dependence on something future or contingent: HOPE. Hebrews 11:1 is perhaps the most quoted verse about hope and faith in the Bible. "Now faith is the substance of things hoped for, the evidence of things not seen." I fear that I have quoted that verse so often with my lips but didn't really take it to heart. It's not just faith, but it is NOW FAITH. Believe it now, hope for it now, and the evidence will follow. Anyone who has lived for any period of time has had hope in something, lost it, and prayerfully — through faith in God and His Word — regained it. What a dark, dismal world it would be without hope in God and confidence in His Holy Word. Proverbs 3:5-6 states it like this, "Trust in the Lord with all thine heart, and lean not unto thine own understanding. In all thy ways acknowledge him, and he shall direct thy paths." Trust, confidence, and hope in their Jehovah were what Abraham and Sarah were going to need as they began the ride of their lives called life.

What would cause a woman to give up her cozy, familiar life and follow someone to the ends of the earth? Love? Maybe. Commitment? Probably. No matter what you are called to do or where you feel led to go, step out with faith and shove the worrisome thoughts of the unknown aside. Love and commitment are necessary, but the truest answer is confidence. An unfailing and unfaltering confidence in the One Who will never lead you astray. Don't know where

UNHAPPY MOTHER'S DAY

you're going? Trust God. Don't know why you're going? Trust God. Don't know when you're going? Again, trust God. He never fails.

Sarah displayed faith in Jehovah and in her husband, and she expected something great from her God. Abram was a mighty man of God with Whom he communed on a regular basis. They were friends according to Isaiah 41:8, "But thou, Israel, art my servant, Jacob whom I have chosen, the seed of Abraham my friend." Knowing Abram's faith in Jehovah, Sarah listened intently to him as he explained God's commandment to leave his homeland. God's commandments are always followed by promises. "Now the Lord had said unto Abram, Get thee out of thy country, and from thy kindred and from thy father's house, unto a land that I will show thee: And I will make of thee a great nation, and I will bless thee, and make thy name great; and thou shalt be a blessing" (Genesis 12:1-2). She had a safe, sheltered life but yearned for God's blessings. Though she was leaving all that was familiar and routine, she knew the man that Abram was, and she expected God to do marvelous things with and through them. They were the world's first power couple. But soon a problem arose seemingly with one of the promises they had been given. A problem that would shake Sarah to her very core and put her trust in Abraham and God in jeopardy.

Have you ever been shaken? Have you had complete faith in someone or something to suddenly have it snatched out of your grasp? I thought I knew absolutely what God's plan was for my life. Number one: marry a preacher. Number two: settle down and be a pastor's wife. Number three: have children and raise them to serve and trust God. Well, when it came to the first one, my plan was spot on. Stan was my best

Wait For It, Sarah

friend, and I couldn't see myself with any one else. Most of our dates were playing 'catch' in the yard or games with my parents. We had fun together. He was my 'preacher man' and best friend.

The second part of my plan was a little skewed, but it turned out fine. Actually, better than fine. God didn't call us to pastor but first to serve in a local church, then to evangelize. That was just an absolute dream come true. I had never been around evangelists, so I didn't know that was a real job. I was amazed that we could travel the country ministering and telling people about Jesus and get paid. Life was progressing even better than I expected because I had always loved to 'go.' When I was little, my mother said that when someone was leaving our house I would say, "Dit my coat." That still is me. I'm always ready to 'dit my coat' and go. I get sand in my shoes if I am in one place for too long. Traveling is in my blood, so to speak.

With the first two parts of the plan playing out almost as I had envisioned, my faith stood firm. It is not hard to follow or believe if you're never questioned or tested, but the third part gave me trouble. I felt like Sarah. I had a promise, but it wasn't being fulfilled when I thought it should be, and my faith fluctuated. Most times it was more of an ebb than flow. Bro. Lee Stoneking put it so perfectly when he said, "Faith is the hand of the soul that reaches out to God and never returns empty." According to Luke 17:6, even mustard seed faith is rewarded: "And the Lord said, If ye had faith as a grain of mustard seed, ye might say unto this sycamine tree, Be thou plucked up by the root, and be thou planted in the sea; and it should obey you." Sometimes I felt that my mustard seed had been ground to dust and scattered in the wind to never return again. Just like a child blowing on a

UNHAPPY MOTHER'S DAY

dandelion. Poof. Gone. Through all of my unbelieving and angry times God was there but never judging. He knew I would once again, through prayer, find that faith that He had given me, and I would use it for His work.

Sarah was the first woman of significance mentioned by name in the Bible after the flood. Because of man's continual sin and refusal to follow in His ways and listen to Him, God had used the great flood as a time of cleansing. Genesis 6:5 says, "And God saw that the wickedness of man was great in the earth, and that every imagination of the thoughts of his heart was only evil continually." Everything had been washed and regenerated. When Sarah reflected on the flood, all things became new in her heart, and Sarah's expectations were just that, new and full of hope. It seemed like there was nowhere to go but up. She expected better things and felt new and refreshed. Abraham and Sarah, trailblazers for a new people and a new way of life!

Time to shed her old nickname. In the land where God was leading them, no one would suspect that, in her homeland, Ur of the Chaldeans, she was known as barren. She had no son to carry on Abram's great name and heritage. How was the promise to be fulfilled if she was infertile? The Bible gives her such a sad title, barren. Webster's dictionary gives the meaning of barren as incapable of producing offspring, but she knew she and Abram were destined for a life filled with children and greatness. Weren't they? God had promised, hadn't He? All she needed was a little patience and trust in Jehovah. Once they reached their promised land, she expected something amazing would befall them, and little did she realize that God's nation and blessed people would come from her. Her road called life may take a few twists and turns, but the promise would stand firm, and she would

Wait For It, Sarah

bear a son that would spawn a nation. We read that now and find it pretty amazing, but remember, she didn't have our Bible to read. She had no idea how her story would end. Sarah would hear the word barren in her mind, and I heard childless. So many times I cried and prayed that God would take that stigma away but feared He never would. Maybe my confidence had been shaky too many times for Him to hear me. Natasha Smith said it so well: "And after you've taken 'it' to Him, leave it there. And by chance, if you happen to pick it up again... take it to Him again. Because God does not grow tired or weary of helping His children."

Actually, Sarah was not originally her name. Sarai became Sarah when God's promise of a son was revealed to her husband Abram. God's promise of a son! Wow, that sounds so fantastic! The promise she had dreamt of for years would finally come to pass. Could it possibly be true? Dare she dream?

Promises are what keeps a person alive and dreaming. Every time I sneaked a peak at a baby magazine, a little bit of light shined through my clouded vision, and a hope of a baby flickered again in my heart. Abram and Sarai's first promise was in Genesis 15:4. God promised their seed would be, "As the stars of heaven." Pretty amazing, but He wasn't finished. Genesis 17:8 declared to Abram, "And thou shalt be the father of a multitude of nations." Abram's name was changed to Abraham during that promise. Now we have Abraham and Sarah. People of God. People of destiny.

Armed with a new name, purpose, and homeland, Sarah was ready for anything. Well, almost anything. She could hardly wait until her promise was fulfilled. As the days turned into months and then years, she would need to

UNHAPPY MOTHER'S DAY

hold on to that promise. She was getting older, but God's Word is always true, and He is always faithful, though we as humans are not. I have had tremendous faith one day, just to flip-flop and tumble into doubt and despair the next. I tend to let my judgment overrule that of God's, and I jump the gun sometimes and make mistakes. My errors didn't have quite as earth-shattering consequences as the one Sarah made, but they were errors nonetheless.

Because she knew God's promise, that a great nation would come from her husband, she thought she would hurry the process along and help God out. She would just bypass the system and become a mother from her maid Hagar. As soon as Hagar conceived, Sarah was despised.

> And he went in unto Hagar, and she conceived: and when she saw that she had conceived, her mistress was despised in her eyes. And Sarai said unto Abram, My wrong be upon thee: I have given my maid into thy bosom; and when she saw that she had conceived, I was despised in her eyes; the LORD judge between me and thee.
>
> Genesis 16:4-5

Now not only was she barren, but she was now despised. That is a far cry from what she expected. She did not have a son as expected, but Abraham had a son with a lowly servant. Anticipation turned to despair when she realized what she had done. Think of the look of pain on her face as she watched Abraham and Hagar's son, Ishmael, interact with them. She would watch those playful scenes and rehearse them a thousand times in her mind. She had

Wait For It, Sarah

not allowed God to work His plan in His time, and now the course of the world's destiny would be changed forever.

I remember one particular service when at altar call a man of God approached me and discreetly whispered in my ear that I would have a son. At that time we hadn't been 'trying' for very long, and I didn't think about it that much, but his words put an expectation in my heart. After several months I became very anxious and uptight, and I began doubting that the minister was even a man of God. That was a very dangerous assumption to make, and if it had not been for the mercies of God I could have strayed from what I was called to do. God forgave my terrible, judgmental attitude, and from that time forward I fervently sought God for a son. There were times that I would be fine, and then the prophecy would come rushing back, and I would be angry and hurt. I really tried rushing God. I actually tried to strong-arm Him at times. Like a spoiled child I would withhold my praise, or 'punish' Him by not reading the Bible or praying. If I could, I would have found a way to rush God's plan just like Sarah. Didn't He know I was ready to be a mother, and I couldn't comprehend why it was taking so long?

Years later I still didn't understand that the prophesy given long ago was supposed to be a comfort to me. A promise that God hadn't forgotten me. I was supposed to look back and find peace and hope, not despair. Eventually, through tears and repentance, I found forgiveness once again for my childish behavior, and I found comfort knowing that He knew all about me, and when the time was perfect, my Isaac would be born. Jane Clayson Johnson said it way better than I: "It takes a lot of faith to put everything you have on the altar of God, trust in Him and know that His plan is better for you than the plan you have mapped out for yourself."

UNHAPPY MOTHER'S DAY

Romans 4:17 speaks of Sarah's womb and says, "(as it is written, I have made thee a father of many nations,) before him whom he believe, even God, who quickeneth the dead and calleth those things which be not as though they were." For so many years I felt the female part of my anatomy was completely dead, but Paul says that He "quickeneth the dead." Sarah's womb may have been dead, but God worked as only He can and brought forth His promised nation. Sarah got her nation, and I got my little angel, Benji.

Two of the most beautiful verses in the Bible are Genesis 21:1-2. "And the Lord visited Sarah as He had said, and the Lord did unto Sarah as he had spoken. For Sarah conceived, and bare Abraham a son in his old age, at the set time of which God had spoken to him." "As He had said" are four of the most wonderful and inspiring words ever spoken. She had a promise, didn't she? He didn't forget her. He just knew that the timing had to be perfect. God knew His plan for Isaac, and sometimes in order to fulfill His complete promise, patience is involved. The last part of Psalm 84:11 says, " No good thing will He withhold from them that walk uprightly." So, now Abraham has two sons by two different women, or does he? The first part of Genesis 22:2 says,"And He said, take now thy son, thine only son Isaac, whom thou lovest." I believe Isaac was Abraham's only son of promise because he was born of Sarah, not Hagar. God gave Abraham and Sarah a promise, and He wasn't going to let Sarah mess it up. He worked around her impatience, and in the end God's perfect plan was fulfilled. God fulfilled His plan in our lives with Benjamin, and I am ever so grateful for that. Pastor Jimmy Toney summed it up this way: "God gave Abraham and Sarah a promise about having a family. It looked impossible. But here's what the Lord said…as the stars in the sky and the sand on the seashore. Whether they were in a season of looking up or one of looking down, both

Wait For It, Sarah

should remind them of His promises."

When our son was placed in our arms I lost my Sarah title. All the years of not-so-patiently waiting vanished. The spoiled attitudes and temper tantrums were forgotten by me, and our merciful, forgiving God. As was the pain of barrenness. God had long since forgiven and forgotten, but oftentimes it takes me longer. Joyce Meyer so accurately said, "Patience is not simply the ability to wait—it's how we behave while we're waiting." I'm so eternally grateful that God didn't reward me with what I probably deserved because of my terrible attitudes at times. I deserved to live my life void of the sound of my son's laughter and the thrill of watching his first steps, but God knew that I was human, and He rewarded me with those beautiful joys and so many more. He has given me a lifetime of happiness with Benji. There is never an excuse for petulance, but the merciful Savior wrapped his loving arms around me and forgave me. I am so thankful that God didn't allow me to interfere. He truly did know who was best for me.

I felt my heart would burst with exhilaration the first time I held Benjamin. I literally felt like Sarah as she stated "God hath made me to laugh, so that all that hear will laugh with me" (Genesis 21:6). The elation I felt as I looked in that little, perfect face was indescribable. I felt Psalm 92:4 to my bones: " For thou, Lord, hast made me glad, through thy work: I will triumph in the works of thy hands." In God's time He made me to triumph, and I became a mother. The singer, Sheryl Crow, said about her baby, "Little souls find their way to you whether they're from your womb or someone else's." That is so beautiful. Benji found his way to me through someone else, but God orchestrated it all and made it perfect. The novelist Gail Tsukiyama was quoted as

UNHAPPY MOTHER'S DAY

saying, "Mothers and their children are in a category all their own. There's no bond so strong in the entire world. No love so instantaneous and forgiving."

It is true that if you rejoice with those that rejoice, your wait time may not be reduced, but it is so worth it in the end. God is faithful to the sometimes unfaithful, and He is true to the often untrue, even to those of us who get impatient and try to rush His timing. Luke 18:1 sums it up, "And He spake a parable unto them to this end, that men ought always to pray, and not to faint." Prayer and faith are the keys to believing for your miracle and becoming strong and eventually victorious over whatever is buffeting you.

The Welsh protestant minister and doctor, Martin Lloyd-Jones stated, " There is nothing which so certifies the genuineness of a man's faith as his patience and his patient endurance, his keeping on steadily in spite of everything." The 'keeping on' is sometimes the hardest part, but keep on we must if we are to embrace our promise. Matthew 24:13 says, "But he that shall endure unto the end, the same shall be saved." When God gave Benjamin to me I was saved from sadness, loneliness, and emptiness, and I was given a life filled with contagious laughter, dirty boy hugs, sloppy kisses, and joy beyond measure. He is a good and faithful God. Don't try to rush Him. He knew your hearts desire before you were even born, and He hasn't forgotten it no matter how long it has taken. The last part of Matthew 6:8 says, "for your Father knoweth what things ye have need of, before ye ask Him." Chances are if He knew before you even asked the question, the answer was already taken care of.

DaySpring Cards founder, Roy Lessin, spoke of having confidence in God like this:

Wait For It, Sarah

*"God is bigger than time,
dates, and appointments.
He wants you to move
through this day with a quiet heart,
an inward assurance that
He is in control, a peaceful certainty
that your life is in His hands,
a deep trust in His plan and purposes,
and a thankful disposition,
toward all that He allows.
He wants you to put your faith in Him,
not in a timetable.
He wants you to wait on Him
and wait for Him.
In His perfect way He will put everything
together, see to every detail...
arrange every circumstance...
and order every step to bring
to pass what He has for you."*

Chapter 7
Who Are You?

UNHAPPY MOTHER'S DAY

You are as much serving God in looking after your own children, and training them up in God's fear, and minding the house, and making your household a church for God, as you would be if you had been called to lead an army to battle for the Lord of hosts.
—Charles Spurgeon

What do you think of when someone says they are alone? Does it immediately cause you to feel sorry for the person who is by himself or herself, or do you just picture them resting and enjoying their surroundings? There is a difference in being alone and lonely. Being alone is having no one else present or to be on one's own. Being lonely is feeling abandoned, forsaken, or rejected. What a difference a couple of letters make in a word. Many is the time that I have been alone with a cup of tea and a good book, reading and feeling at peace with myself and God. I felt as if I didn't have a care in the world and could stay that way for hours. The world and all it's cares just had to wait and let me recharge my batteries, so to speak. But, other times I have been at a conference or church service surrounded by hundreds of people, and felt more lonely than anyone could ever imagine. I would watch these happy people and even interact with them, but couldn't shake the feeling of abandonment. I know He is always with me, but I just couldn't shake the feeling of aloneness. Isolation can happen whether you are by yourself or in a crowd, and believe me it is no respecter of persons. Perspective is a powerful thing. Do you have a tendency to see the cup as

Who Are You?

half empty or half full? Missionary and author Pearl S. Buck put it beautifully: "Inside myself is a place where I live all alone and that is where I renew my springs that never dry up." Sometimes we just need to be alone to renew our spirits and attitudes.

Loneliness has a way of gripping your very heart and soul and refuses to let go. If it is left unattended it will strip the very life and strength from you, but Zephaniah 3:17 gives us hope saying, "The Lord thy God in the midst of thee is mighty; he will save, he will rejoice over thee with joy; he will rest in his love, he will joy over thee with singing." When we read this verse we know that God is right in the middle of our loneliness and is going to save us from ourselves. We will still have to face issues, sometimes without human intervention, but God is always there. Our mighty God is certainly in the midst of us.

If you truly look in people's eyes, you can see that many hurting souls are going through things much worse and need someone to talk to, but loneliness says to lock your feelings up inside. Don't say a word. You don't matter to anyone, and your hurt and loneliness are the only things you can think of right now. No way their pain is equal to yours. Your pain and grief are the most important issues, and their's can take a back seat. I ugly cried more times than I can list, and the quote from picturequotes.com was truly accurate, "Invisible tears are the hardest to wipe away." Because I felt invisible, my tears must have been also. Looking back, not caring about others feelings sounded so callous, but 'soul pain' is like that, and a good cleansing from God is the only thing that will heal it. For me it took several trips to the altar before it was completely gone, and once in a while when I thought I had it under control, I would peek at a baby and

UNHAPPY MOTHER'S DAY

it would rear its ugly head, and back to the altar I would go, repenting. Try as you may, you can't cover up 'soul pain.' As a girl I got in the most trouble for my dirty looks. I attempted to cover up what I was actually thinking. I was too smart to spout off to my parents, but if looks truly could kill, I would have been an orphan many times over. I always thought that maybe if I'd smile and go my way, one day I would wake up, my problems would vanish, and the sun would shine again. Psalm 62:8 reassures us, "Trust in him at all times; ye people, pour out your heart before him: God is a refuge for us. Selah." He is our safe place. In a refuge, or safe place, confidences are made, promises are kept, and pain is left on the outside. There is no better place for the lonely than in God's refuge. Psalm 46:1 promises, "God is our refuge and strength, a very present help in trouble." He gets right in there with us.

Loneliness makes a person feel invisible to everyone, and I felt especially forsaken in a room full of happy, chatting, new mothers. Nursery duty in church was the worst. I did it because it was my duty, but I would rather clean every bathroom in the church, without gloves, than play with a baby. Older kids were okay, and I can't even begin to explain that, but babies were a different story. All the happy-mom talk just isolated me and made me feel as if I were in a foreign country. What was that language they were speaking? Bottles, burp pads, breastfeeding, blah, blah, blah. Friends and family who loved me, and even God Who made me, seemed to look right through my soul. When spoken to, I would smile and try to be pleasant, and repeat what I had heard my sisters-in-law say about the whole baby process, but I screamed on the inside, "I couldn't care less about your feeding times and sleep patterns. Leave me alone and let me feel sorry for myself in peace." That is terrible and embarrassing, but loneliness enveloped and choked

Who Are You?

the breath out of me. I tended to forget Isaiah 41:10, "Fear thou not; for I am with thee: be not dismayed: for I am thy God: I will strengthen thee; yea, I will help thee; yea, I will uphold thee with the right hand of my righteousness." He sees you, and knows where you are, and one day the sun will shine, and the dark cloud of loneliness will lift, and you will be alive, happy, and breathing again. I love the first part of Psalm 68:6, "God sets the lonely in families." That is such a powerful verse for anyone struggling with feeling invisible and longing to have a child. Families come in all different sizes: lots of children, only one or two, and maybe none at all. I didn't realize that I was already in a family with Stan. God made us a family in 1986.

So many great men in the Bible come from powerful, incredibly-visible women. Solomon, the wisest king of Israel, was mothered by Bathsheba. She overcame the pain of loss of a husband and child only to realize the joy of motherhood again. She was named in the lineage of Jesus. Moses, the deliverer of Israel, was born of Jochabed. It was she who was bold enough to rebel against Egyptian law and risk death to save her son. God allowed her to raise her son for Pharaoh's daughter and lead him in His truths. Mary, the mother of our Lord, endured more than any of us would ever dream. Even before she watched her firstborn, promised child crucified, she was ridiculed, shamed, and called unspeakable names. Yet she bore the Savior of the World, Jesus. These men must have been proud to have strong, amazing women as their mothers. Women who guided and helped mold them into men of God. Women who were so important that they, along with their beautiful stories, were mentioned by name in Gods Word. These ladies are preached about and celebrated, and in Sunday school, as children, we are taught most aspects of their remarkable lives.

UNHAPPY MOTHER'S DAY

This brings us to Samson: a man among men. He was truly a mighty man, stronger than anyone, and the last judge of Israel. I've seen little boys flex their muscles and pretend to be him in Sunday School. He performed many powerful feats and proved himself many times over to his fellow Israelites. His mother must have been someone amazing. The Bible tells us that his father's name was Manoah, and his mother's name was .... Wait a minute, I'll think of it in a second. Her name was .... I give up. I just can't think of it. I looked it up but couldn't find it. Who was she?

Samson's mother's name is never mentioned in the Bible. Judges 13:2 states, "And there was a certain man of Zorah, of the family of the Danites, whose name was Manoah; and his wife was barren, and bare not." The first description we have of her is that she was barren. There is that ugly word—barren—again. No name, just an adjective, barren. She must have been pretty special though for the Almighty God to send an angel down to her, not just once but twice. Not many people in the Bible can testify to that happening. God must have known she was a strong woman who could bear a strong boy. The angel said unto her in Judges 13:5, "For, lo, thou shalt conceive, and bear a son; and no razor shall come on his head: for the child shall be a Nazarite unto God from the womb: and he shall begin to deliver Israel out of the hand of the Philistines."

After the angel appears to Manoah, and his wife reassures him that death is not imminent, Judges again states it beautifully in chapter 13 verse 24, "And the woman bare a son, and called his name Samson: and the child grew, and the Lord blessed him."

'The woman bore a son.' After such a glorious

Who Are You?

happening, it seemed so impersonal. After all that, she was still nameless and invisible. She did what God had called her to do, no matter how hard. She was held to a higher standard and was commanded not to eat or drink certain things, and her reward, other than her wonderful, mighty son, was anonymity. She was faithful and obedient and was rewarded as such. Her name need never be mentioned, because her legacy speaks for itself. The woman who was once labeled as barren was now the mother of a judge and deliverer. In a mighty way she had made a name for herself.

2 Kings 4:8 speaks of a 'great woman.' She and her husband, who was also unnamed, tended to the needs of Elisha, the prophet of Israel. Each time he passed through Shunem, he knew he had a place of refuge. After his long, dusty travels he could always count on a private, relaxing room to call his own and a home cooked meal to fill an empty stomach: the biblical equivalent of today's evangelist's quarters. I know first hand what a powerful blessing they are to an evangelist's family. She had urged her husband, "Let us make a little chamber, I pray thee, on the wall; and let us set for him there a bed, and a table, and a stool, and a candlestick: and it shall be when he cometh to us, that he shall turn in thither" (2 Kings 4:10).

Could it be she knew the hardships that Elisha faced as he traveled teaching her people the words and ways of God? She had a servant's heart and wanted to ease the burden of the man of God. God had blessed her and her husband, and she in turn desired to bless God's prophet.

I'm assuming that her husband was much older than her, because the Bible mentions that he was old, but there is no mention of her age. He was more than likely past the age

UNHAPPY MOTHER'S DAY

to father children, and she had probably resigned herself to the fact that she would not have a baby. Perhaps it was an arranged marriage as was the custom of that day. Her heart and hands were open and giving, yet her arms were empty.

Elisha wanted to repay this faithful woman who eased his and his servant, Gehazi's burdens, so informing her of that, he said, "About this season, according to the time of life, thou shalt embrace a son. And she said, Nay, my lord, thou man of God, do not lie unto thine handmaid" (2 Kings 4:16). She couldn't bear to get her hopes up again. The very next verse confirms what Elisha said: "And the woman conceived, and bare a son at that season that Elisha had said unto her, according to the time of life" (vs 17). It was true. She had her beloved child, and that would lead to one of the biggest miracles in the Bible. Imagine her joy of watching him learn, grow and prosper. There is nothing like waiting for years, then watching your child's 'firsts.'

Years passed, and she faced one of the most challenging times of her life, for the child had fallen ill and died. God once again proved Himself faithful and true when He caused Elisha to raise him up and restore him to his mother, the Shunammite woman. She was blessed not once, but twice. She wasn't called by a given name, just the nickname given to her by the prophet: a great woman. Nameless, yet again, oh so blessed! She was blessed by not one but two miracles from her beloved Jehovah! It was Nakeia Homer who wrote, " Behind every strong woman is a story that gave her no other choice." Sometimes we have no other choice than to be strong.

Two things tormented me while on my infertility journey. Baby showers and Mother's Day. I cannot count

Who Are You?

the number of showers I attended in the 12 1/2 years we wanted a baby. By around year eight my smile was glued on, and my responses were memorized like part of a poem. "I am so happy for you guys!" "I hope you have a boy/girl too." "Well, some day we will have a baby, we're just enjoying life right now." That was the most outrageous line of them all. I was NOT enjoying life right now. I was incomplete. Like sewing a garment without material, or reading a book without words. I wanted to laugh sarcastically and then scream to the top of my lungs. There were times after the silly shower games and all the hooplah that I went home, threw myself on the bed, and wept for hours. I should have, but got little comfort from Psalm 147:3, "He healeth the broken in heart, and bindeth up their wounds." I knew it was true but just couldn't get past the hurt and emptiness. Could these people not see that I was dying inside? I wanted a baby more than anything, and every baby shower I attended I became a little more invisible. No one saw my hurt and pain. I had a shattered heart, but no one saw me. Quotepixel.com sums up my feelings adequately: "It would be too easy to say that I feel invisible. Instead, I feel painfully visible and entirely ignored."

Mother's Day. The worst two words in the English language! It went way beyond dislike. The strongest word I can think of was fury. I hated those words with every fiber of my being. I had the absolute best mother on the planet, but because of our travel schedule I was rarely with her on that day, coupled with the fact that I longed for a baby, made it a miserable day. While we were traveling, it took all the courage I could muster just to get dressed and attend church. Faithfulness had been drilled into me from the day I prayed through as a teenager, but that was the one day of the year I struggled. I knew I had to go but was determined to disassociate myself during service. As a minister's wife

UNHAPPY MOTHER'S DAY

I was usually seated up front and had to once again paint that pleasant, fake grin on my face. I felt like the biggest hypocrite in the world. "Would all the mothers please stand and let us recognize you?" each preacher would say, then they would pass out the gifts as I disappeared while still seated on my pew. I never took one unless it caused an uncomfortable moment. One church I attended handed out huge hanging plants to all the mothers, which was fine until he called me on the platform for mine. I was embarrassed and felt humiliated. I wanted to disappear into the carpet and remain there for the rest of the service. No one there had a way of knowing that we wanted a baby, but I felt ashamed that I had taken something that I didn't deserve. I went back to our trailer pouting and purposed to not water the plant. It didn't die quickly enough. Poor plant. It had to suffer for my tantrum. How could a person feel invisible and so conspicuous at the same time? Seemingly, I was the only lady usually not standing on that special day. My husband always looked at me from the platform, and the love on his face said it all. I wasn't invisible to him. I was loved beyond measure and knew, though dealing with his own pain, he would do anything to take mine away. Men and women suffer differently, but make no mistake about it, men do suffer. My hurt and pain was no greater than his.

I knew that God loved me, and I felt, perhaps, He looked at me the same way Stan did. The last part of Psalm 139:18 says, "When I awake, I am still with thee." And Isaiah 49:16 states, "Behold, I have graven thee upon the palms of my hands." I matter to Him. I'm right there in His hands where He is holding and protecting me. He sees me! I can rest assured that He always knows where I am, what I am feeling, and always sees me. Even in my weakest hours. Even when I have ugly feelings, and feel like the world around me is collapsing, He knows my name.

Who Are You?

Another person who knows my name is my son, Benjamin. Oh, how I longed for a child for years, and the minute he was placed in my arms and those beautiful brown eyes looked at me for the first time, I knew I was no longer invisible. The first time he said "Mama," my heart melted. He has always seen me for who I am: his mommy. Because of a wonderful, masterful God Who has always seen my grief, I now have the greatest blessing in the world. A wonderful son to lead and guide in the ways of the Lord. The words of the psalmist David were so true when he penned "Lo, children are an heritage of the Lord" (Psalm 137:3).

In the Book of Nehemiah, the Israelites were being counted after the wall was built, and chapter seven verse 66 says, "The whole assembly together was forty and two thousand three hundred and threescore, besides their menservants and their maid-servants, of whom there were seven thousand three hundred thirty and seven: and they had two hundred forty and five singing men and singing women." That shows me that while it is important to be front and center, and be used of God in ministry and singing, it is more important to be a servant. No, servants are rarely seen, and there is not much glory in cleaning the church, wiping noses in Sunday School, or picking up trash in the parking lot, but God sees, and I feel that it is just as important to serve the church, your husband, and family as it is to be in front of thousands in a beautiful cathedral. Myron Wideman Jr. said, "God can take a nobody and make them a somebody in front of everybody without asking anybody."

George Eliot once said, "The happiest women, like the happiest nations, have no history." Seemingly, these women had no history, but just as 'the Shunnamite woman' and 'the woman' allowed their names to be hidden, they

UNHAPPY MOTHER'S DAY

played a very important part in writing history. Your arms may still be empty, and you may feel that you are invisible, but never give up. God has a plan for you, and you matter to Him. Let Him have your hurt and pain. You are visible and one day will make an amazing mom. You and your child will write a wonderful history book full of love and adventure. English actress Helen Barry said, "Good things come to those who wait. Better things come to those who never give up and the best things come to those who believe." So true, Helen, so true.

You may be facing a different circumstance today besides infertility, and you may feel alone, inadequate, and insufficient, but you are not invisible. God sees you and knows exactly where you are. Maybe only God knows what you've been praying for, but guess what? He is the only One that matters. In His time He will fulfill your dreams and wishes. Maybe your dreams need to be altered a bit to fit His will, and if you are willing, you, too, can make it happen. Jennifer Hudson said, "Sometimes God makes better choices for us than we could have ever made for ourselves." He is trustworthy, so let's trust Him.

Chapter 8

Tick Tock, Elizabeth

UNHAPPY MOTHER'S DAY

*Motherhood is priced of God, at price no
man may dare to lessen or misunderstand.
—Helen Hunt Jackson*

Can you imagine being Elizabeth, wife of Zacharias, cousin to Mary the mother of Jesus? Zacharias was kind of a big deal in his town. He was not only a priest after the order of Abia, but also, "righteous before God." As a matter of fact, he and Elizabeth were both called righteous in the Bible. Luke 1:6 says, "And they were both righteous before God, walking in all the commandments and ordinances of the Lord blameless." People looked up to and respected them. I honestly can think of no other word I would rather be called than righteous. Other words for righteous are: virtuous, moral, and upright. Zacharias and Elizabeth were all of these and more. After 400 years of Jehovah's silence, they were included in a small band who had never left their heritage and hope of a Messiah. Their holiness and faith was refreshing and very needed. I imagine they yearned to hear from the One True God. They knew promises in the Scriptures and knew His coming was imminent. They had watched the signs and been faithful to their God and each other. Little did they know what part they would play in His divine plan. Other than a handful of faithful people, the Jewish people, for the most part, had forgotten they needed a savior. Little did I know that a wonderful adoption agency would become that same thing for me and Stan. Our Savior used them as a savior for us and many people. Years of deafening silence was about to be replaced with glorious, beautiful praise! Praise in the form of baby giggles and lots of love.

Tick Tock, Elizabeth

Elizabeth was a descendant of Aaron, the first priest of Israel. As the brother of Moses, and his mouthpiece, Aaron helped lead the Israelites out of the bondage of Egypt. Imagine the faith it took for Aaron to follow Moses. He hadn't heard the voice of Jehovah but was trusting his runaway brother, hoping and praying that what Moses said God instructed them to do was the right thing.

Growing up in the shadow of such mighty ancestors must have set a tremendous example for Elizabeth of how a man or woman following God should live. What an awesome heritage she had. Elizabeth was taught daily the commandments of Jehovah and also His promises. Deuteronomy 6:6-7 says, "And these words, which I command thee this day, shall be in thine heart: And thou shalt teach them diligently unto thy children, and shalt talk of them when thou sittest in thine house, and when thou walkest by the way, and when thou liest down, and when thou risest up." By the time Elizabeth was ready to be given in marriage, she knew to base her whole life on God and His Word. She may have spent her entire childhood and adolescence preparing for her future life to please her Jehovah first and her husband next. I imagine she was yearning for the time she could "teach them diligently unto her children." She had led a faith-filled life up until now and knew that God would lead her in His ways. I had not been raised in this truth, but once I got the Holy Ghost I was ready to live my life all in for Him and couldn't wait to see what God had in store for me. I went from wanting to be a women's professional basketball player to a preacher's wife just like that.

In Bible times, women had arranged marriages, so Elizabeth really had no say about her future, but she knew her beau's family would be of the same, fine lineage and importance as hers to the Kingdom of God. She was marrying a high priest. What did God have in store for such a chosen couple? Even before Zacharias and Elizabeth were married, they knew they were each called to work for the Kingdom. As a high priest he burned incense when he went into the temple, and she tended to the needs of their home. With no children to raise, I'm sure she had many lonely days because of her husband's service to Jehovah in the temple. Lonely days to sit and dream about the future of babies and happy times. A house of one tends to be empty, but, she thought, soon all that would change. Because Stan spent most weekends traveling and ministering with the singing group, I knew about empty rooms and arms. I felt lonely but knew I was never truly alone. Mandy Hale beautifully says, "A season of loneliness and isolation is when the caterpillar gets its wings. Remember that next time you feel alone."

The Bible doesn't give us the specifics of their married life, except they were prayer warriors. Luke 1:10 states, "And the whole multitude of the people were praying," and in 1:13 an angel says, "Fear not, Zacharias, thy prayer is heard." The angel alludes to the fact that he had prayed for a son. Because of their lives of ministry, sacrifice, and prayer, God had some wonderful days ahead but before all the excitement was loneliness and heartbreak. Heartbreak — year after long year. Childlessness was considered a stigma in those days, and many may have thought it was because one of them had sinned, but we know differently because God had a plan. Barren women were judged harshly back then, but God was going to do something bigger and mightier than had been seen in a very long time. It had certainly been a while since Elisha or Elijah had performed a miracle, but the time was right, and God had set things in motion for the greatest miracle of all time. The motivational speaker and author, Wayne Dyer, put it simply, "I am realistic — I

Tick Tock, Elizabeth

expect miracles."

    Some people are labeled as beautiful or smart. Some are industrious or wealthy. Those are fine tags, but in todays society, not every label is flattering. They now have to be politically correct to avoid offending anyone, but any label, no matter how correct it appears to be, is still a label. When I was in my late teens I was painfully shy, but I was known as a 'stuck up.' Once I got to know someone better, we usually became fast friends. Now, I try to force myself to make the first move and hopefully the 'stuck up' label has become a thing of the past. If not, I can only work on myself and not worry about what others think.

    Elizabeth was known face-to-face around town as "righteous," but I'm sure "barren" was hurtfully whispered behind her back. She was meticulous in her duties around the house, but she was barren, She managed the servants with ease while Zacharias was away, but she was barren. Her main duty to her husband was to have children, but because of her barrenness she could not. It seemed easy and natural enough, but somehow she could not bear him a son. A common practice in Old Testament times was for a husband to either divorce his wife or find another to fulfill her duty of childbearing, but Zacharias, being a righteous man who loved his wife, trusted Jehovah to give them their desire. He looked to their ancestors Abraham and Sarah for encouragement, but like them, they were getting on up in years. They would soon be too old for children, but how old was 'too old' for God? Thankfully, He doesn't work on our time table, or pay attention to man-made labels.

    The uplifting titles of righteous and blameless now gave way to another title for Elizabeth: well stricken in

UNHAPPY MOTHER'S DAY

years. That, perhaps, is the saddest of all. Once age takes a firm hold there seems no hope. Her youth was fading right before her eyes, and she was helpless to change it. There were no miracle fertility drugs or special treatments in those days, just trusting on nature to take its course. In other words, once she heard 'well stricken in years' she must have felt old and useless. She was getting too old to even hope. She knew she was quickly reaching the age where childbearing was impossible. We don't know how old she was, but the average age of childbearing is from 12—51, so imagine the pain and shame Elizabeth felt to be past the age of childbearing. Year after year of watching her peers bear and raise children. Then having grandchildren to spoil and love. Not having a man child to carry on the family name was just not acceptable. Would their lineage cease because of her? Having a man child was her one job: the reason she felt she was created. It is sad to say that sometimes we pin all our hopes and dreams on one goal, and when it is not reached by a certain self-appointed time, we feel like failures. Athletes work in a certain time frame to reach perfection. When a certain age is passed, the hopes for their goal is dashed. No trophies, no rings, no series wins, and for an old childless woman—no babies. Sometimes we completely forget God's perfect timing. Her husband had trusted her, and she had let him down. She thought, perhaps he should have chosen a different woman. Can you relate? I could. I felt guilty because I knew Stan would make a great daddy, but I just couldn't produce. The sad fact was that Elizabeth had no control over it, and as much as she longed to give Zacharias a son, her old body just would not cooperate. What a feeling of helplessness and hopelessness, but little did she know that God was working behind the scenes for them. God was ministering to her husband while Zacharias was ministering for Him. Elizabeth had no idea the angel Gabriel had appeared to her husband with the promise of a son!

Tick Tock, Elizabeth

When I look back, I can now see that my loving, faithful Lord had worked behind the scenes on my behalf also. When Stan and I married, I was pretty young and immature, so there were certain things God needed to accomplish in me that He just couldn't until I was older and ready. God did me a huge favor by not giving me a baby right away, but I couldn't see that until many years later. The immature me was old, barren, and even at 30 I felt 'well stricken in years.'

Zacharias finally returned from the temple, but something strange had happened to him. He was not only changed in spirit, but he couldn't speak! Elizabeth soon learned the reason and found she was going to have a baby. Finally, a son! What a blessed time they had preparing for their promise. The spring came back in her step, and the song returned to her heart. The townsfolk knew just by their countenance that something was happening with Zacharias and Elizabeth even before they could see the evidence. Elizabeth's prayers had been answered right on time. She sure didn't feel like a 50 plus year old. She was expecting a special child! The same angel that visited them stopped off to see Mary the mother of Jesus. When Mary saw Elizabeth the Bible says, "And it came to pass, that, when Elizabeth heard the salutation of Mary, the babe leaped in her womb; and Elizabeth was filled with the Holy Ghost" (Luke 1:41). The whole, wonderful thing was confirmed. It was truly a miracle. Luke 1:37 states it perfectly: "For with God nothing shall be impossible." Absolutely nothing! Elizabeth's faith was rewarded, and the course of history was set. She traded all the old names to become Elizabeth the "mother" of John.

I was Elizabeth. I was a 34 year old woman whose biological clock had just about stopped ticking. It had slowed to a crawl, and I had almost given up. Unlike a clock,

UNHAPPY MOTHER'S DAY

though, I couldn't rewind or speed up the time. My chance of conceiving was rapidly decreasing along with my spirits. My doctor said that, other than a few minor gynecological issues, he could see nothing wrong with me. There was no reason I couldn't conceive. (Later, when I was diagnosed with autoimmune issues, my problem was discovered.) The doctor had several clinical, cold and rehearsed answers ready. Maybe I was trying too hard. Relax and enjoy your husband and marriage. There is always plenty of time. No rush, he said. That was easy for him to say as he went home to his busy family. His children met him at the door with hugs and giggles. My dog met me with a wet nose and sometimes an unwelcome present. I wanted to laugh at him and run out of the office screaming, "I've tried that. Give me answers!" But I quietly left, went home, and cried all day, finally falling asleep with a wet pillow—only to wake up the next morning feeling hopeless, empty, and still childless.

I had just about anything I wanted. A fantastic, loving husband, and a great family with dozens of friends. We traveled the country full time and saw many beautiful sights that God created. I should have been enjoying the ride, and I still did to a certain extent, but there came a time when none of that mattered. Phil 4:11 says, "Not that I speak in respect of want: for I have learned, in whatsoever state I am, therewith to be content." I tried to be content doing what God wanted us to do, and I loved being with Stan and traveling. I just felt old and empty. I struggled with the fact that I was becoming old and still childless. Sometimes, inadequacy and worthlessness smothered me like a blanket. I wanted a baby more than anything. I met friends along the way that were in the same boat as me, and we formed a bond. Just to know that someone else was having the same struggles somehow made it a little more bearable. Acts 2:44 says, "And all that believed were together, and had all things

Tick Tock, Elizabeth

common." Martin G. Collins explains it like this: "Godly unity produces joy because it overcomes the sorrow of self-seeking and fulfills the true love of outgoing concern for others. Joy through unity comes when God's people have all things in common—the same beliefs and desires working toward a common goal." We had a common goal alright. Becoming a mother and eventually holding our angels. We wept, prayed, and dreamed together. It is true that there is strength in numbers. Psalm 130:5 seemed to be our battle cry, "I wait for the Lord, my soul doth wait, and in his word do I wait." Wait—that was all we could do. Wait, hope, pray, and believe that someday we would be among the women blessed enough to be called mom.

Some of the kids I taught at the Christian school were grown and married and beginning to start their own families. I became more upset as the days progressed. I truly loved those girls and boys, but I just didn't understand why not me. I attended dozens of their baby showers and watched while my friends snuggled and cuddled their babies. That did nothing to help my situation, and it was getting to be more than I could bear. I was getting too old and could do nothing about it. Girls my age or older who married after me were having children. It was almost too much. How many more years would I have to watch others enjoy what I so desperately wanted? I put on a happy face and was happy for them, but a little piece of my heart broke every time I saw them adoring those little faces God had blessed them with. Psalm 13:1-2 states what I thought perfectly: "How long, O Jehovah? wilt thou forget me forever: How long wilt though hide thy face from me?" I really felt forgotten. Many years had passed since the wonderful prophecy God gave to me. God never gave me a time-frame. I did that to myself. Sometimes I draw that line in the sand and expect God to cross it and make all my dreams come true.

UNHAPPY MOTHER'S DAY

We had prayed and sought counsel from our pastors, and we applied for adoption. If this was the route God wanted to take us, we were willing, and actually became excited again. The time spent waiting was just like when we first talked about starting a family. We were full of excitement and anticipation again and began dreaming and planning. God had breathed new life into us, and we were again looking forward to our future family.

Sometimes, even when you're expecting something, you are still amazed when it happens, and that was the way it was with us. We knew the call would come but weren't expecting it when it did. Finally, just like as with Zacharias, an angel called us. Not Gabriel, rather, it was the beautiful director of the adoption agency, Debbie Velie. She had our little man and he was waiting for us. Our promise was finally fulfilled. I remember standing in our travel trailer when Stan came in with the news. Without him telling me I knew instantly that it was a boy. He was tiny, cuddly and all ours. Just like Elizabeth, God came through and gave me my "John." I felt like a giddy school girl with a new toy. He was amazing, and I couldn't stop laughing and crying. God had done it. He had fulfilled His promise to me. It wasn't the way that I had planned, and it sure wasn't when I thought it should have been, but it was perfect timing. The second they called us, I was a mother. I never had any doubt about it, and Benjamin was my son.

According to Ecclesiastes 3:1, "To every thing there is a season, and a time to every purpose under the heaven:" Psalm 1:3 says, "And he shall be like a tree planted by the rivers of water, that bringeth forth his fruit in his season, his leaf also shall not wither, and whatsoever he doth shall prosper." Just as in nature, our lives continually go through

Tick Tock, Elizabeth

seasons. God has planned it that way. Nothing would grow correctly without spring, summer, winter, and fall. Elizabeth and I both had our seasons. My favorite season is summer, and anyone that knows me knows that I don't like winter at all, but summer's warmth wouldn't be so wonderful if I didn't have to endure the frigid cold of the winter. It was the same way with my childless season. I'm not sure I would have savored every moment of motherhood had it come earlier in my life. Perhaps I would have been too busy working or being a newlywed wife. God knew that I needed to wait on His perfect timing to get every bit of enjoyment out of my 'summer.' He not only knows what's best for us, but He also knows when is best for us. Timing is everything. The Puritan poet Anne Bradstreet wrote, "If we had no winter, the spring would not be so pleasant: if we did not sometimes taste of adversity, prosperity would not be so welcome." So true.

Patience is a 'trying' word. I have never been accused of having much, and when I was a young girl, I got in trouble for not using the patience I did have. Patience means: "the capacity to accept or tolerate delay, trouble or suffering without getting angry or upset." I remember very few times in my life that I just 'rolled with the flow' and not become irritated at the delay, whether it was going on a family trip or learning to share a toy or treat. As I grew older I learned to at least control my impatience and deal with life's speed bumps. I never liked to hear anyone quote that verse in Luke 21:19 that says, " In your patience possess ye your souls," because I was afraid the Lord would come while I was having a tantrum and my soul would be lost. During the first 12 years of our marriage I clung to Jeremiah 29:11, "For I know the plans I have for you, declares the Lord, plans to prosper you and not to harm you, plans to give you hope and a future." Nothing God ever does is for our harm or

UNHAPPY MOTHER'S DAY

detriment. He loves us and would never intentionally hurt us. What He does is for our good and should make our faith grow and stretch our lives.

God is amazing. Always remember that it's never too late. Don't ever give up no matter what your head or body says. He may not have answered according to my original plan, and yes, I was a little older than most mothers, but He gave me the perfect baby boy in His perfect time. Christian author Jim Cymbala said, "Faith never denies reality but leaves room for God to grant a new reality." Maybe I wasn't as ready when I was young as I thought I was. Maybe I have more patience now. Whatever the reason, I know He is ever faithful. He didn't forget me or Elizabeth, and He certainly won't forget any promise He gave to you. Hold on to Psalm 138:3: "In the day when I cried thou answerdest me, and strengthenedst me with strength in my soul." Just as God had restored the dry bones in the book of Ezekiel, He restored Elizabeth's womb and my faith. He is the giver of life and strength. Receive strength and life in Jesus name.

Gils Exposition of the Entire Bible says it this way: "Hope deferred maketh the heart sick....That is, the object hoped for, if it is not enjoyed so soon as expected, at least if it is delayed any length of time, the mind becomes uneasy, the heart sinks and fails, and the man is dispirited and ready to despond, and give up all hope of enjoying the desired blessing: whether it be deliverance from any evil, or the possession of any good;" In all reality I saw myself as too old to have a child, but God saw me as just the right age. I'm so thankful that His timing is not ours and I have enjoyed my blessing since I gazed into those piercing brown eyes.

What do you need? What are you asking God for?

Tick Tock, Elizabeth

Has He not answered the way you want or when you want? He is never too late, and He never forgets your prayer request. Consider Lazarus, Mary, and Martha. The siblings faced the trial of their lives. Lazarus was gone, and the sisters were devastated, but they didn't have to worry because their best friend was a miracle worker. They saw healings with their own eyes. They called for Him, and He should be here soon. No, that was not the case. Four days. Four days, mind you. If it were me I would have been mad and said just forget it. Well, the sisters didn't, and Jesus sure didn't. Four days late is not too late for our God. Four days, four months, four years, or centuries doesn't matter. Give it to God.

Chapter 9

My Miracle Is Here!

UNHAPPY MOTHER'S DAY

*Motherhood is a million little moments that
God weaves together with grace, redemption,
laughter, tears and most of all, love
—Lisa TerKeurst*

Jeremiah 33:3 states, "Call unto me and I will answer thee, and shew thee great and mighty things, which thou knowest not." How many years did we call upon the Lord for our need? We really didn't see it as a 'great and mighty' thing, just one small tiny person to make our family complete. Stan and I loved each other and Him, but still felt so empty and incomplete. We had no idea that on one particular day this verse would come to pass not in a mighty, earthshaking way, but in a teeny, squirming, beautiful way. The 'things which we knew not' were about to rock our world!

The call! The call that forever changed our lives happened on an ordinary spring day. We were preparing for our Wednesday night service and planning the rest of our week's services and traveling schedule. Working for and with the Tupelo Children's Mansion kept us busy with sales, sponsor forms, and love gifts, besides the presentations and ministry part. We knew God's ministry was a huge responsibility and were determined to give it our all. God's Kingdom deserves nothing less. Psalm 100:2 instructs His church to "Serve the Lord with gladness." I felt it was not hard doing that when I was doing what I loved with the person I loved. We felt God had called us to this life and we enjoyed traveling, visiting new churches, and making new friends. We always wanted to do our best for the Kingdom

My Miracle Is Here!

of God, and we couldn't wait to share our wonderful life with a little one. We certainly weren't expecting anything out of the ordinary that day.

We had just rolled into a new town to hold a series of services in and around the area. We pulled our home behind us, and I always felt like it was my doll house. Actually, being with Stan made every place we ever lived home. I began straightening the inside of our travel trailer which was my job when we first arrived at a new place. Just because it wasn't a conventional house didn't mean that it wasn't home, and I took pride each time I tidied up inside. I set up all the pictures of family and other things we brought to make it feel more homey, and Stan was out running errands, which he always did after taking care of the outside set-up. The two of us had a perfect system: I was the homebody that tended to our physical needs, and he was the planner, organizer, and grocery shopper. It seemed to work perfectly for us. We had a service that night, so we had little down time. If I had too much time my mind would wander down the childless road and would begin to feel melancholy. I knew God was ever faithful and IN HIS TIME our promise would be delivered.

For 12 1/2 years we had done everything in our power that we felt we should do to have a baby, with no results. Every month began with high hopes and expectations and ended with tears and frustration. We trusted the Lord and felt we should get pregnant naturally. Not that there is anything wrong with other ways, we just felt that those were not right for us at that time. We were told by many well meaning friends to obey Exodus 14:13, "Stand still and see the salvation of the Lord," and Psalm 46:10, "Be still, and know that I am God:" I felt like most of the time

UNHAPPY MOTHER'S DAY

we honestly tried to do that, but sometimes we stood so still that we felt like the earth's natural forces were moving us backward. Life was great, but disappointments kept backing us up. We loved our life on the road but still dreamed of how perfect it would be if we had a little one to share the adventure with. We dreamed of visiting zoos, museums, and parks as a little family. The two of us explored every new area, but we couldn't wait to show our child God's wonderful creations.

As I mentioned before, Stan had gone out to get a few groceries and items for our trailer. He wasn't gone long, which was strange because it was a fairly large city, and he enjoyed price comparing and finding bargains, when I heard him pull up. I went outside thinking perhaps something was wrong with the vehicle, but when he stepped out of the van he had an odd look on his face. Right before our eyes, Numbers 23:19 was coming to pass: "God is not a man, that he should lie; neither the son of man, that he should repent: hath he said, and shall he not do it? or hath he spoken, and shall he not make it good?" I have to admit that through the years of our struggle my faith did waver many times, but I am ever so thankful that God indeed sees our hearts and knows we are all too human, and He forgives our failings. Stan told me he had received a call from the adoption agency, and if we were ready, our baby was waiting to meet us. If we were ready? What? Are you kidding me? I felt as if I had been ready my whole life. Like Esther I was born for 'such a time as this.' I had always said that I didn't care the sex of the baby as long as it was healthy. It's funny that instantly, without Stan saying a word, my heart knew we were getting a boy, and immediately my head started spinning with possible names. We could barely contain our excitement. With one phone call seemingly out of the blue, Matthew 19:26 became a reality in our lives. "But Jesus beheld them and said unto them, With men this is impossible: but with God all things are possible."

My Miracle Is Here!

God never does anything 'out of the blue,' and I believe we were destined to be a family from the beginning. I think it just took a while because God was making sure all parties were truly ready. Benji needed us, but we sure needed him more. David Platt explained it this way: "It's important to realize that we adopt not because we are rescuers. No. We adopt because we are rescued." I felt as if I had been stuck in a terrible storm and suddenly a bright shining beacon led me to safety. Motherhood was my safety.

We excitedly talked non-stop all that afternoon, and with counseling we decided that no matter how bad our flesh wanted this, we would pray about it for 24 hours and then give them our answer. I had to ride herd over my flesh because I didn't want to pray about it, because I was afraid God would change our minds, and I sure didn't want to wait 2 hours more less 24. I wanted that baby! My heart said yes, yes, yes, but my head said that I really did want God's will for our lives and that precious boy's life. If He wanted us to wait longer, then wait we would, but I'm telling you that was the longest 24 hours of my life. My heart was already committed, and I really felt that this was His will, but I was obedient and honestly prayed for God to guide us. During the service for TCM I'm embarrassed to say that I have absolutely no idea what Stan preached or sang. All I could do was dream about diapers, formulas, pacifiers, and most of all holding my little man. I imagined his sweet baby smell and the relief I would feel once he was in my arms for good. Stan was up there preaching, but I was already out shopping.

We let our pastor and parents know about the possibility of a baby, and they were praying with us. After talking, dreaming, and planning most of the night, we felt it was God's will to adopt this little one. Honestly, we only

UNHAPPY MOTHER'S DAY

waited 23 hours and about 55 minutes to call them. I hope that wasn't cheating God, but my heart was going to explode if we didn't call. The funny part was that the office staff at the agency knew that we were going to say yes, and they had already overnighted pictures of him which we received just a couple hours after our call. This was way before cell phone photos, so they wanted us to have them the next day. When I saw that perfect, beautiful face, my heart melted, and I finally exhaled. That perfect little pink creature was my boy, and I was his mom. Oh, my word! I was a MOM. I think I had been holding my breath for a couple days.

Our baby boy! Wow, that was music to our ears. I always wondered what I would do and how I would react when I got the news. Now I knew. It almost seemed as if I was in a slow-motion dream but didn't want to wake up. I had to keep reminding myself that it wasn't a dream and it was completely a reality. My baby, my boy, my son. I just couldn't quit saying it. Now to pick the perfect name. Proverbs 22:1 states, " A good name is rather to be chosen than great riches, and loving favor than silver and gold." All during church that night I scoured the Bible. Because he was a gift from God it had to be biblical. It needed to be strong sounding but go well with Cook. After a few minutes I found the perfect one, Benjamin, son of the right hand. After Benjamin—in the Bible—was born, he needed a new mommy, and my Benjamin did too. Benjamin, Ben, Benji. They all sounded like music to my ears, and of course I could think of no better middle name than Stanley. I wanted to name him after his daddy; therefore, Benjamin Stanley Cook came to be. Pure perfection.

Because of previous commitments on our end, as well as the agency, we couldn't pick him up for a few days,

My Miracle Is Here!

which gave us plenty of time to prepare ourselves and our travel trailer. When he saw his new home it had to be perfect. It is crazy how many things a baby requires. When we started buying, our trailer filled up pretty quickly. A church we were preaching at the next weekend found out about our baby and threw a surprise shower for us. God's people are absolutely the best, and Benji received so many beautiful things. Our trailer was parked near a major city, so we spent our days scouting out stores for just the perfect items we thought we needed. The baby bed had to fit in a small space and his clothes in cute little baskets. We picked up more than we needed but couldn't help ourselves. The thought of our son compelled us to shop. The ladies who were his foster mom's were so thoughtful and took pictures every day, starting at two days old. We put some of the pictures which were sent us in an album, and the others we placed on our nightstands so we could wake up to his sweet face every morning until we could wake up to the real thing. Every restaurant and store we went in we would tell them our story and show them the pictures. Some people may have thought we were crazy, but we really didn't care. We were walking on cloud nine and enjoying every step. Everyone was so nice and acted like they really cared. You won't believe the free food we received!

The time was approaching, and we were nervous, afraid, and excited. Could we be the kind of parents he needed? We were older now, so how would we have the energy to keep up with him? God knew our fears and trepidation and told us in Isaiah 41:13, "For I the Lord thy God will hold thy right hand, saying unto thee, Fear not; I will help thee." If He is holding our hand and guiding us, how could we go wrong? Psalms 56:3 also told us, "What time I am afraid, I will trust in thee." God's promises have never failed and will never fail us, so we were confident that

UNHAPPY MOTHER'S DAY

He was the Proprietor of our lives, and He would guide and care for all three of us. We were still a bit nervous but knew this was of the Lord, and we were ready to get our baby.

We had a Tupelo Children's Mansion service in Ohio the night before our big meeting day, and as usual, Stan did an awesome job, and God blessed, but my mind was oh so far away. We never wanted to rush the Lord, and we tried to never let it matter what we had going on because a move of God was the most important item on the agenda. However, I did get very impatient during service a time or two, and I hurriedly packed up our sales items after the last customer. The pastor knew our plans, so we didn't do the customary fellowship after church, and we just changed our clothes and headed out. We had decided that because of our late start that we would stop half way to spend the night in order to be fresh for our meetings the next afternoon. We chatted nonstop about everything from bottles to bibs. We really didn't know what we were talking about completely, but we were dreaming and imagining our life as parents. We were ready for our dreams to become our reality. I couldn't believe that after all the pain filled years this was really happening, and with every passing mile the excitement built. I felt I was going to burst with anticipation.

Stan had made up a song that he sang all the way there. "Benji is my baby boy, Benji is my pride and joy, makes me smile and oh so glad, makes me proud that I'm his dad." He beamed every time he sang it, and I have never felt so content in my whole life as I did during that late night trip to get our son. I wasn't a singer/songwriter so I just hummed lullabies.

Each passing mile we became more pumped up, and

My Miracle Is Here!

by the time we passed the half way mark we just decided to drive all the way to the town. I don't think we were driving. Floating is actually what it was. We had blocked off a section of rooms for our family at a local hotel and called them to see if we could get in early, perhaps paying for an extra night. The manager was so nice and could sense our excitement so much so that he gave us a room in the wee hours of the morning without a charge. God has had his hand in everything we have done so far. He cares about even the smallest detail of our lives. Matthew 7:11 states, "If ye then being evil, know how to give good gifts unto your children how much more shall your Father which is in heaven give good things to them that ask him?" Good things just kept on happening.

Finally, after we checked in and rested a while and made sure we had everything in order, we began getting ready. I was so nervous that I sliced my finger open on a razor when I stuck my hand in my overnight bag. I think I was even more anxious than the day I got married. It absolutely wasn't cold feet, I just wasn't sure I had what it took to be a mom. I listened for years how every expectant woman talked and sang to her womb, and I didn't get that opportunity. Was I really going to be a mother who could guide her boy in God's ways? I had prayed for him for all these years, and I felt My Saviors' reassurance that He had ordained all this, and He was in control of Stan, me, and Benjamin.

Revelation 21:4 summed up my feelings perfectly: "And God shall wipe away all tears from their eyes, and there shall be no more death, neither sorrow, nor crying, neither shall there be any more pain for the former things are passed away." I realize that is talking about something

UNHAPPY MOTHER'S DAY

totally different, but that is how I felt. Until you have lived a childless life, you can't imagine pain and tears. I've heard it said that for all of the women that complain about stretch marks, there are a dozen who would love to have them.

We pulled into the parking lot, and I think I got out almost before the van stopped. I was so excited, but I composed myself before I headed in with Stan. After small talk, it was time. The moment the foster mom placed that little black-haired doll in my arms, the pain of the last 12 1/2 years melted away. We seemed to lock eyes, and I immediately felt Benji accept me as his mom. I can't even explain the emotions I felt. Total mind-boggling awe and wonder. It was the most profound peace I have ever felt in my life. God is amazing, and I want to never underestimate His power. I read this by Kay Arthur and it is so true, "God is in control, and therefore in EVERYTHING I can give thanks—not because of the situation but because of the One who directs and rules over it."

The women that handed him to me kept remarking that they were amazed that I was so calm while signing the papers and during the briefing about his habits and needs. I felt an overwhelming peace. I held my tears and emotions in check because things needed to get done. I didn't want any snags or loopholes to jeopardize our new family. After all the paperwork and pleasantries, we calmly placed 'our son' in his new car seat and proceeded to put him in the van to take him to meet the rest of his family who were anxiously waiting at the hotel to love our little bundle of joy. When I heard Stan click his car seat in place, it hit me that I am now officially a mother, and the floodgates opened. The reality of our decision hit home, and I couldn't stop the tears. 12 1/2 years of pain, anger, bitterness, and heartache were washed away, and tears of joy and relief flooded my soul. After so many years of dreaming and planning, it was a finality. God had answered our prayers and 'mommy and daddy and baby finally made three.' The Apostle Paul speaks of the faith of Abraham in Romans 4:20-24. "He staggered not at the promise of God through unbelief: but was strong in faith, giving glory to God; And being fully persuaded that, what he had promised, he was able also to perform. And therefore it was imputed to him for righteousness. Now it was not written for his sake alone, that it was imputed to him; But for us also, to whom it shall be imputed, if we believe on him that raised up Jesus our Lord from the dead." Did you read that? BUT FOR US ALSO! I love that. I sometimes thought when I read of the barren ladies in the Bible who received their promises, that it was only for them. I wasn't like them, so I couldn't get what they got. They were super spiritual, super heroines. But God inspired Paul to tell me that God would do it for me. Little ole' me. If He will do it for me, who is totally unworthy, He will surely do it for you. I'm ashamed to say that I did stagger at the promises of God from time to time, and I did have some unbelief at times, but I also always knew that He was able and would perform in His time.

Keep believing, trusting, and praying. God has you and your need in the palm of His hand. The last part of Hebrews 11:11 sums this book up perfectly when it says about Sarah giving birth to Isaac: "Because she had judged him faithful who had promised." Faithful—that is the perfect word for our God.

I love this quote by Mark Batterson: "You'll never be a perfect parent, but you can be a praying parent. Prayer is your highest privilege as a parent.... Prayer turns ordinary

UNHAPPY MOTHER'S DAY

parents into prophets who shape the destinies of their children, grandchildren, and every generation that follows.... Your prayers for your children are the greatest legacy you can leave."

God has been faithful through the ages. All these years later I still feel overwhelmed by God's faithfulness. Every morning of Benjamin's existence I have praised God for him, and as with everything in life there are ups and downs, but I will never forget where God brought me from.

Throughout those several years of childlessness I had many, many people praying for me. Some I know prayed daily. At all the times I felt so alone, I now realize that I never was. I know I had an army of prayer warriors who surrounded me and fought for me on their knees. When I felt like giving up and throwing in the towel, their prayers urged me on. I feel like we are family today not only because of God, but also His people. Ecclesiastes 4:9-12 was my theme: "Two are better than one; because they have a good reward for their labour. For if they fall, the one will lift up his fellow: but woe to him that is alone when he falleth; for he hath not another to help him up. Again, if two lie together, then they have heat: but how can one be warm alone? And if one prevail against him, two shall withstand him; and a threefold cord is not quickly broken." There is no way I could have endured this journey by myself.

If you are on this infertility trip, remember that you are not alone. As you already know, God is there, but so are His saints. Don't isolate or insulate yourself. One can't be warm alone, and when you stumble, which you will, it is much harder to raise yourself up. I realize now that my 'cord' must have been a whopper. A Japanese proverb

My Miracle Is Here!

says it this way, "A single arrow is easily broken, but not ten in a bundle." Rev Joel Urshan said, "I've never preached about just Shadrach or just Meshach or just Abednego, but I have preached several times about Shadrach, Meshach, and Abednego. There's something about people going through the fire together that creates an inseparable bond which links them forever."

If you are watching a loved one travel the lonely road of barrenness, you have an important role in their lives. There is nothing that can physically be done to help them, except these three important things:

> Being there: If you know your sister is going through an especially rough stretch, invite her to lunch or shopping. No, that won't make the problem disappear, but it helps just knowing someone cares.

> Just listen: Please don't tell them you know what they are going through unless you have actually gone through it yourself. You have no idea of the very real feelings of pain and anguish.

> Don't judge: Every time I had ugly and hateful thoughts, I knew I was wrong. I didn't need someone to state the obvious and make me feel worse. I already hated myself for the pangs of bitterness that oftentimes overwhelmed my heart.

Those three simple things are just as much a part of ministering for the Kingdom as preaching and teaching to the lost, because during those rough times we feel lost! Isaiah 40:1 gives this commandment: "Comfort ye, comfort ye my people, saith your God."

UNHAPPY MOTHER'S DAY

If perhaps infertility is not your issue, but some other malady or problem is, and you have prayed unceasingly for an answer, as I stated earlier in this book, there are three answers—yes, no, and wait. Our answer was wait, but perhaps your answer is a no. God is still faithful. I have had several noes in my life; still, God loves me enough to know what is best for me, and faithful enough to give me some important yeses. I'm sure not saying it is easy, but He will keep you, and He always has something better. Honestly seek for the better. You may never truly understand, but through faith and obedience to Him, your testimony could be an inspiration to others. Evangelist Tim Chandler preached a message that included this: "People say, 'If it's God's will it will happen.' That's NOT true! Noah spent 120 years building an ark and only eight souls were saved. You think that was God's will? No! There are a lot of things God wants to do in our lives, but sometimes we stand in the way with our selfishness. We have the ability to interfere in His will. God is in charge, but He is not always in control." The first part of Hebrews 12:2 says, "Looking unto Jesus the author and finisher of our faith;" He wrote the first chapter of your life when you were conceived, and He will write the conclusion when your life is done. Everything in between is meticulously crafted by our Lord. He won't write a few words and then go silent on you. There may be times He is quieter than others, but He is always there writing your story.

This has been my story. It was not intended to do anything except give glory to God. I have exposed my weaknesses and left myself vulnerable, but through all my spiteful, hateful, bitter and sometimes sinful attitudes, God was there. I did nothing on my own except repent and honestly seek His counsel and guidance. Deep in my heart I really always wanted what was best for me and my husband. If God had chosen to never give me a child I know He would

My Miracle Is Here!

have given me peace and strength to continue on that path, BUT I am ever so thankful for His blessing of a son. To God be all the glory! A poet—who's name remains a mystery—once wrote:

> "A mother's heart and a mother's faith
> And a mother's steadfast love
> Were fashioned by the angels
> And sent from God above."

My baby boy now has a baby boy, and for many years I never dreamed I could be a mama, more less a Nana. I just can't get over God's faithfulness. As I hold my grandson, Banz Exander Cook, my mind floods with memories of Benjamin Stanley Cook and their similarities. Our sweet God allows me each day to relive my boy's childhood. Psalm 145:4 declares, "One generation shall declare thy works to another, and shall declare thy mighty acts."

I always want Benji to know this beautiful and oh so true quote from Fleur Conkling Heyliger: "Not flesh of my flesh, nor bone of my bone. But still miraculously my own. Never forget for a single minute, you didn't grow under my heart but in it."

So, I may not have had times in my life that I was as jealous as Hannah, betrayed like Rachel, impatient like Sarah, felt invisible and nameless, and finally, too old like Elizabeth. But my God was oh so patient and loving. He saw me through some tough times, and He was right by my side during this crazy rollercoaster ride. Let Him walk right beside you and guide you. I promise you won't be sorry. You'll have peace like you have never known. Psalm 23:6 says, "Surely goodness and mercy shall follow me all the days of my life, and I will dwell in the house of the LORD forever." No matter life's twists and turns, if you will allow Him to follow you, you will be at peace dwelling in His grace.

Special Thanks

Some special people put their time and prayers into this book, and I'm ever so appreciative.

I want to thank my Mom, Erlene Coutcher, for always being my sounding board. She saw me through many temper tantrums and helped me pray my way out of them. I couldn't have done it without you and Dad.

Thank you to Larry Arrowood and the Woodsong Publishing team for believing in this project and putting their time and effort in publishing.

Special thanks to Jeremy Hart for designing a beautiful cover. I didn't really give you much to work with, but you did an awesome job.

Thank you to Sister Debbie Velie for having a burden for adoption and putting the right baby with the right home.

I thank God for seeing my tears and fears. You knew exactly what You were doing, and I should have known all along that the answer was just wait. You taught me patience while You were preparing the perfect baby. You made our family complete. I could never thank You enough.

Quote References

Motherhood is priced of God, at price no man may dare to lessen or misunderstand. Helen Hunt Jackson, featured in Helen Hunt Jackson Quotes

Only God Himself fully appreciates the influence of a Christian mother in the molding of character in her children. Billy Graham, Brainy Quotes

Motherhood is a million little moments that God weaves together with grace, redemption, laughter, tears, and most of all, love. Lysa TerKeurst tweet

Parenting begins the moment you make any conscience effort to care for your own health in preparation for enhancing your child's conception. Carista Luminare-Rosen found on Instagram, Oct 22, 2019

You are as much serving God in looking after your own children, and training them up in God's fear, and minding the house, and making your household a church for God, as you would be if you had been called to lead an army to battle for the lord of hosts. Charles Spurgeon, The Complete Word of Charles H. Spurgeon, Volume 23 Sermons 1331-1390 Delmarva Publications, Inc

Your greatest contribution to the kingdom of God might not be something you do, but someone you raise. Andy Stanley, found on Pinterest

No calling is greater, nobler, or more fulfilling than that of motherhood. Sally Clarkson, The Mission of Motherhood, WaterBrook, 2003

Mothering is the gospel lived out as you hold your child's heart in beauty, prayer, and patience. It's not the big decision, but the little ones, trusting God through it all. Elizabeth Hawn, Choices of Life Resource Center

Jesus taught that providing shelter for the shelterless, food for the hungry, and clothing for the naked are sacred acts. They're also the hallmark activities of mothering. When we do them from the right motive for those in our homes, it's as if we've done them for Christ Himself. (Matt. 25:31-45) Jen Wilkin, Encouraging Truth About Motherhood, Pinterest

I remember my mother's prayers and they have always followed me. They have clung to me all my life. Abraham Lincoln, Goodreads

Almost every sinful action ever committed can be traced back to a selfish motive. It is a trait we hate in other people but justify in ourselves. Stephen Kendrick, Readbeach

Delayed does not mean denied, God is just giving you a moment of silence to prepare for what He's about to do in your life. Bishop T.D. Jakes, Retweeted by Toby Mac

Faith is the hand of the soul that reaches out to God and never returns empty. Lee Stoneking

Faith sees the invisible, believes the unbelievable, and receives the impossible. Corrie Ten Boom, Quotefancy

Never be afraid to trust an unknown future to a known God. Corrie Ten Boom, Brainy Quote

The God who created names and numbers the stars in the heavens also numbers the hairs of my head. He pays attention to very big things and very small ones. What matters to me matters to Him and that changes my life. Elizabeth Elliot, Elizabeth Elliot Quotes at AZQuotes.com

God is in control, and therefore in EVERYTHING I can give thanks—not because of the situation but because of the One who directs and rules over it. Kay Arthur, AZQuotes

Faith never denies reality but leaves room for God to grant a new reality. Jim Cymbala, Quotefancy

Godly unity produces joy because it overcomes the sorrow of self-seeking and fulfills the true love of outgoing concern for others. Joy through unity comes when God's people have all things in common—the same beliefs and desires working toward a common goal. Martin G. Collins, The Thinking Mind

Little souls find their way to you whether they're from your womb or someone else's. Sheryl Crow, American Adoptions as posted on Pinterest

You can only be jealous of someone who has something you think you ought to have. Margaret Atwood, The Handmaids Tale, Knopf Doubleday Publishing Group, 1998, Goodreads

Loss is nothing else but change, and change is Nature's delight. Marcus Aurelius, Brainyquotes.com

Faith deals with the invisible things of God. It refuses to be ruled by the physical senses. Faith is able to say, 'You can do what you like, because I know God is going to take care of me. He has promised to bless me wherever he leads me.' Remember that even when every demon in hell stands against us, the God of Abraham remains faithful to all his promises. Jesus Christ can do anything but fail his own people who trust him. Jim Cymbala, Fresh Faith, Zondervan, 2011

I have not failed, I've just found 10,000 ways that won't work. Thomas Edison, Brainyquotes.com

It takes a lot of faith to put everything you have on the altar of God, trust in Him, and know that His plan is better for you than the plan you have mapped out for yourself. Jane Clayson Johnson, crackermuffin@blogspot.com

God is bigger than time, dates, and appointments. He wants you to move through this day with a quiet heart, and inward assurance that He is in control, a peaceful certainty that your life is in His hands, a deep trust in His plan and purposes, and a thankful disposition, toward all that He allows. He wants you to put your faith in Him, not in a timetable. He wants you to wait on Him and wait for Him. In His perfect way He will put everything together, see to every detail… arrange every circumstance… and order every step to bring to pass what He has for you. Roy Lessin, AZQoutes

You are the poem I dreamed of writing. The masterpiece I longed to paint… You are the shining star I reached for In my ever hopeful quest for life fulfilled. You are my child Now with all things I AM BLESSED. Anonymous, Goodreads.com

A season of loneliness and isolation is when the caterpillar gets its wings. Remember that next time you feel alone. Mandy Hale, Goodreads.com

Invisible tears are the hardest to wipe away. Picture quotes.com

It would be too easy to say that I feel invisible. Instead, I feel painfully visible, and entirely ignored. QuotePixel.com

Great is thy faithfulness! Great is thy faithfulness! Morning by morning new mercies I see All I have needed thy hand hath provided Great is Thy faithfulness, Lord unto me! Pardon for sin and a peace that endureth, Thine own dear presence to cheer and to guide; Strength for today, and a bright hope for tomorrow Blessings all mine, with ten thousand beside. Thomas Chisholm, Public Domain

Our prayers may be awkward. Our attempts may be feeble. But since the power of prayer is in the One who hears it and not in the one who says it, our prayers do make a difference. Max Lucado, Goodreads.com

You know you're in love when you can't fall asleep because your reality is finally better than your dreams. Dr. Seuss, Goodreads.com

The secret of a happy marriage is finding the right person. You know they're right if you love to be with them all the time. Julia Child, Brainyquotes.com

What is the use of praying if at the very moment of prayer, we have so little confidence in God that we are busy planning our own kind of answer to our prayer? Thomas Merton, Thoughts in Solitude, goodreads.com

God knew that it doesn't matter how your children get to your family. It just matters that they got there. Kira Mortenson, Adoption.org
A strong woman is one who feels deeply and loves fiercely. Her tears flow as abundantly as her laughter. A strong woman is both soft and powerful, she is both practical and spiritual. A strong woman in her essence is a gift to the world. Native American saying, dailyinpirationalquotes.com

Once you embrace your value, talents, and strengths, it neutralizes when others think less of you. Rob Liano, Goodreads.com
There is nothing ordinary about you. You are a DAUGHTER OF THE KING, and your story is SIGNIFICANT. Lisa-jo Baker, Proverbs 31 Ministries

Jealousy is counting someone else's blessings instead of your own. Anonymous

Betrayal is never easy to handle and there is no right way to accept it. Christine Feehan, Rising Above Trauma-Infidelity, 2021

Impatience can cause wise people to do foolish things. Janette Oke, Goodreads.com

Many of the bravest never are known, and get no praise. [But] that does not lessen their beauty. Louisa May Alcott, quotepark.com

Aging is not lost youth but a new stage of opportunity and strength, Betty Friedan, brainy quote.com

One day you will tell your story of how you overcame what you went through and it will be someone else's survival guide. Diane Sowerby, Carrots'n' Cake, 2021

A single arrow is easily broken, but not ten in a bundle. Japanese proverb

Mothers and their children are in a category all their own. There's no bond so strong in the entire world. No love so instantaneous and forgiving. Gail Tsukiyama, Goodreads.com

And she loved a (not so) little boy very, very much, even more than she loved herself. Shel Silverstein, The Giving Tree, Pinterest

You won't always be strong but you can always be faithful. Dwight Fulton

I've never preached just about Shadrach or just Meshach or just Abednego, but I have preached several times about Shadrach, Meshach and Abednego. There's something about people going through the fire together that creates an inseparable bond which links them forever. Joel Urshan

The strength people are not those who show strength in front of the world but those who fight and win battles that others do not know anything about. Johnathan Harnisch, Goodreads.com

Behind every strong woman is a story that gave her no other choice. Nakeia Homer, Nov 14, 2020 Twitter

God can take a nobody and make them a somebody in front of everybody without asking anybody. Myron Wideman Jr., funny.com

Complaining about a silent God while your Bible is closed, is like complaining about not getting texts when your phone is turned off. 95.1shinefm

When it feels like you're empty and hurting alone know that God is present in this space with you and as you draw near to Him He will draw near to you, He sees what no one sees, He hears what isn't said but is cried out by the heart and He will restore you. Brittney Moses, Goodreads.com

We can always find something to be thankful for, and there may be reasons why we ought to be thankful for even those dispensations which appear dark and frowning. Albert Barnes, Brainyquote

I am realistic—I expect miracles. Wayne Dyer, Goodreads.com

If we had no winter, the spring would not be so pleasant: if we did not sometimes taste of adversity, prosperity would not be so welcome. Anne Bradstreet, PassItOn

Breathe, darling. This is just a chapter, not your whole story. S C Lourie, tinybuddah.com

Insecure people only eclipse your sun because they're jealous of your daylight and tired of their dark, starless nights. Shannon L. Alder, Goodreads.com

The most important lesson that I have learned is to trust God in every circumstance. Lots of times we go through different trials and following God's plan seems like it doesn't make any sense at all. God is always in control and he will never leave us. Allyson Felix, Allyson Felix Quotes

Anger, resentment and jealousy doesn't change the heart of others—it only changes yours. Sharon Alder, Goodreads.com

Good things come those who wait. Better things come to those who don't give up and the best things come to those who believe. Helen Barry, Quotespedia.org

It's important to realize that we adopt not because we are rescuers. No, we adopt because we are rescued. David Platt, AZQuotes.com

CPSIA information can be obtained
at www.ICGtesting.com
Printed in the USA
LVHW052112090123
736780LV00001B/228